O F

–

BUILDING YOUR OWN SUSTAINABLE AND ENERGY EFFICIENT HOUSE

BUILDING YOUR OWN SUSTAINABLE AND ENERGY EFFICIENT HOUSE

Henry Skates

THE CROWOOD PRESS

First published in 2011 by
The Crowood Press Ltd
Ramsbury, Marlborough
Wiltshire SN8 2HR

www.crowood.com

British Library Cataloguing-in-Publication Data
A catalogue record for this book is available from the British Library.

ISBN 978 1 84797 258 3

The right of Henry Skates to be identified as the author of this work has been asserted by him in accordance with the Copyright, Designs and Patents Act 1988.

Dedication
To Janessa, Rebekah, Lewis and Rachael for their patience in waiting for this book to be finished while our own house remained unfinished.

Typeset by Jean Cussons Typesetting, Diss, Norfolk

Printed and bound in India by Replika Press Pvt Ltd

Contents

Chapter 1   Introduction 6

Chapter 2   Project Management.. 17

Chapter 3   The Site.. 32

Chapter 4   Planning Permission.. 43

Chapter 5   Purchasing Your Plot... 52

Chapter 6   Sustainable Design – a Holistic Approach 60

Chapter 7   Design for Energy Efficiency 75

Chapter 8   Building Regulations.. 95

Chapter 9   Finance, Tenders and Contracts................................ 107

Chapter 10   The Construction Process 120

Chapter 11   Project Completion 141

Appendix: Case Studies... 150

Further Information.. 187

Index.. 188

CHAPTER ONE

Introduction

The introduction sets the tone of the book. It begins with a compelling argument for building in an energy-efficient and sustainable way based on cost, human comfort and environmental issues (not least of which is climate change). It then provides an overview of the various stages that are involved in the design and building process. It concludes by outlining a range of sustainability measures that should be considered at an early stage to ensure that these can be incorporated at minimum cost and to maximum environmental performance.

WHY BUILD A SUSTAINABLE HOUSE?

If you could build a house that was comfortable all year round, just the right size; not too hot in summer not too cold in winter, plenty of natural light and well ventilated without feeling a draught – just right in fact – would you be interested? What if you could build such a house and heat it and maintain it for minimal cost for the life of the house? What if you were able to build the house in a sustainable way using sustainable materials and minimize its environmental impact? What if you were able to build such a house and it cost only fractionally more than a conventional house to build, would you still be interested? All of this is possible but only if, when building your own house, you ensure that sustainability is considered broadly at the outset and then in detail at appropriate stages in the development of the design.

In doing this you will minimize not only the cost of building but also the running costs and you will maximize the environmental performance of the house, making it a home that is a pleasure to live in. It is not sufficient to first design a house, build it and

The author enjoying the fruits of his labour.

then try to add sustainability by bolting on as many sustainable technologies that you can afford. Many sustainability measures can be implemented at little cost and some measures can be implemented at no additional cost. It is worth noting right at the outset that the costs associated with building a sustainable house will significantly increase if sustainability advice is received or applied too late in the process.

Before we address what you can do to make your proposed home as sustainable as possible, it is worth reminding ourselves of the wider issues at stake. If the above reasons are insufficient in their own right, there are other more pressing reasons for why we need to build in a sustainable way. Global warming is now a generally recognized phenomenon and sustainability is now widely recognized as being a necessity, not an option. One of the main culprits blamed for global warming is carbon-dioxide (CO_2), so it is worth taking a look at what can be done about it. CO_2 is produced by each of us every day, and our personal carbon footprint is a measure of how many tonnes of CO_2 are emitted, directly or indirectly, as a result of our consumption of goods and services. In the United Kingdom the average person's CO_2 production is around twelve tonnes per annum. The government initially set a target to reduce CO_2 to eight tonnes per person per annum by 2010, but studies have shown that to be truly sustainable, the average emissions should be closer to two tonnes of CO_2 per person per annum. In effect, this means that when building your house you should take every opportunity to build in the most sustainable way so as to minimize your own carbon footprint. The fabric of your house however, is not the only culprit in contributing to CO_2 production.

There are three main areas in general in which we contribute to carbon emissions and these relate to our lifestyle, our transport and of course, our houses. Our lifestyle in the western world is one in which we consume vast amounts of both raw materials and energy in the production of goods. We have more than we need and we consume more than we need. In the process of doing so we generate vast quantities of CO_2 and other pollutants and also vast quantities of waste that normally goes to landfill. If we want to reduce our carbon footprint we need to consume less. When it comes to transport, approximately half of the population owns or has access to a car and around one third of our CO_2 production is transport related. The average emissions related to CO_2 production from transport are around two tonnes of CO_2 per person per annum, which means that on transport alone we expend what should be our full quota of CO_2 production. This means that the location of your house will have an impact on how much transport related CO_2 you are responsible for. Our homes themselves are also responsible for approximately one third of our total CO_2 production. The UK government has at last recognized the impact that house building has on CO_2 production and has stated that by 2016 all new homes must be built to be zero-carbon. In order to achieve this every new house will be required by law to be much more sustainable.

MAKING SURE YOUR HOME IS SUSTAINABLE

The Bruntland Report definition of sustainability is the one most often quoted: 'meeting present needs without compromising the ability of future generations to meet their own needs'. The problem is however that this is a very broad statement and does not really help the self-builder to decide on exactly what it is that you can do to build a sustainable home. The task is made more difficult by the plethora of products on the market making claims as to how sustainable they are. Questions immediately arise such as which materials should you choose and which technologies should you employ in your new home, and how can you measure the overall sustainability of a particular design? Thankfully, there are now a number of well established and comprehensive methods of measuring just how sustainable a project really is. One such method is The Code for Sustainable Homes developed by the Building Research Establishment. For some exponents of sustainable design, the Code does not go far enough, but it is one recognized measure whereby you can gauge just how sustainable your house will be.

The Code for Sustainable Homes

The Code for Sustainable Homes is a voluntary standard that was introduced in the UK in April 2007 and has become compulsory for all government-

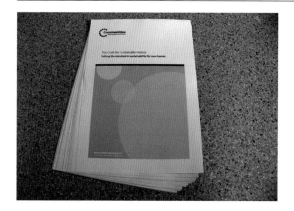

The Code for Sustainable Homes.

funded housing. The overall objective is to promote the design and construction of new homes to higher environmental standards. The stated purpose of the Code is to measure the overall sustainability of new homes by providing a single framework within which the house building industry can operate.

The Code measures the sustainability of a home against nine different design categories before rating the 'whole home' as a complete package. Each category includes a number of environmental issues that have an impact on the environment. The issues are assessed against a performance target and awarded one or more credits. These performance targets have been set to represent good or best practice, and are designed to be achievable by the building industry as a whole. This means that they should be easily achievable for the dedicated sustainable self-builder.

The design categories and the issues associated with the component parts are listed below, as are the objectives behind each of the environmental issues. They are listed here at the outset of this book to raise your awareness of the issues that need to be considered before you begin to design your sustainable home. If your house has already been designed, then you should incorporate as many of the issues as you can to try to make your house as sustainable as possible.

The Code for Sustainable Homes uses a sustainability rating system from one to six stars depending on the extent to which it meets the performance targets. One star is the entry level and represents a

standard just above the level of the 2007 Building Regulations. Six stars is the highest level representing exemplar development in terms of sustainability and should be your goal if possible. At the very least, you can use the above as a checklist to ensure that you or your designer has given due consideration to each of the issues listed. Some of the issues, such as daylighting, can be incorporated at no cost; others, such as extra insulation, may incur a little more capital cost, but will pay for themselves many times over during the lifetime of your home. Then again, others will incur additional capital cost and may have very long payback periods, but if you want to build in a sustainable way, you will give due consideration to each measure.

WHAT ELSE IS INVOLVED IN BUILDING A SUSTAINABLE HOME?

If you are serious about building your own energy-efficient and sustainable home, then there are a number of recognized stages involved in the process. They may not occur in such a linear fashion as outlined below, and there will be a number of overlaps between stages, but it is a reasonable guide for what to expect.

The Initiation Stage

Every self-build house project begins with the idea that you would like to build your own house. You may not know much about sustainability, or building for that matter, but if you go through with the process you will soon become something of an expert.

Research and Information Gathering
Early in the process you will engage in research and in gathering as much information about the project as possible. You will need to identify a site and make arrangements to purchase it if it is suitable for your needs.

This stage of the process includes (but is not limited to) gathering information about the site such as location, ownership, site boundaries, local context, topography and site features, local climate and so on. It is useful to have this information at hand before

Design Category	**Energy and CO$_2$ Emissions**
Environmental issue	Dwelling emission rate (mandatory)
Objective	To limit emissions of carbon dioxide (CO$_2$) into the atmosphere which arise from the operation of a dwelling and its services.
Environmental issue	Building fabric
Objective	To future-proof the energy efficiency of dwellings over their whole life by limiting heat losses across the building envelope.
Environmental issue	Internal lighting
Objective	To encourage the provision of energy-efficient internal lighting, thus reducing the CO$_2$ emissions from the dwelling.
Environmental issue	Drying space
Objective	To provide a reduced energy means of drying clothes.
Environmental issue	Energy-labelled white goods
Objective	To encourage the provision or purchase of energy-efficient white goods, and so reduce the CO$_2$ emissions from appliances in the dwelling.
Environmental issue	External lighting
Objective	To encourage the provision of energy-efficient external lighting, and reduce associated CO$_2$ emissions.
Environmental issue	Low or Zero Carbon (LZC) technologies
Objective	To reduce carbon emissions and atmospheric pollution by encouraging local energy generation from renewable sources to supply a significant proportion of the energy demand.
Environmental issue	Cycle storage
Objective	To encourage the wider use of bicycles as transport by providing adequate and secure cycle storage facilities, thus reducing the need for short car journeys.
Environmental issue	Home office
Objective	To reduce the need to commute to work by providing residents with the necessary space and services to be able to work from home.
Design Category	**Pollution**
Environmental issue	Global Warming Potential (GWP) of insulants
Objective	To reduce global warming from blowing agent emissions that arise from the manufacture, installation, use and disposal of foamed thermal and acoustic insulating materials.
Environmental issue	NOx emissions
Objective	To reduce the emission of nitrogen oxides (NOx) into the atmosphere.
Design Category	**Water**
Environmental issue	Internal water use (mandatory)
Objective	To reduce the consumption of potable water in the home.
Environmental issue	External water use
Objective	To encourage the recycling of rainwater and reduce the amount of mains potable water used for external water uses.
Design Category	**Heath and Wellbeing**
Environmental Issue	Daylighting
Objective	To improve the quality of life in homes through good daylighting and to reduce the need for energy to light the home.
Environmental issue	Sound insulation
Objective	To ensure the provision of improved sound insulation to reduce the likelihood of noise complaints from neighbours.

Roof lights are a good method of ensuring good daylight penetration deep into the plan.

Environmental issue	Private space
Objective	To improve the occupiers' quality of life by providing for their use an outdoor space which is at least partially private.
Environmental issue	Lifetime homes (mandatory)
Objective	To encourage the construction of homes that are accessible to everybody and where the layout can easily be adapted to meet the needs of future occupants.
Design Category	**Materials**
Environmental issue	Environmental impact of materials (mandatory)
Objective	To encourage the use of materials with lower environmental impacts over their lifecycle.
Environmental issue	Responsible sourcing of materials – building elements
Objective	To recognize and encourage the specification of responsibly sourced materials for the basic building elements.
Environmental issue	Responsible sourcing of materials – finishing elements
Objective	To recognize and encourage the specification of responsibly sourced materials for the finishing elements.
Design Category	**Management**
Environmental issue	Home user guide
Objective	To recognize and encourage the provision of guidance to enable home owners/occupiers to understand and operate their home efficiently and to make the best use of local facilities.
Environmental issue	Considerate constructors' scheme
Objective	To recognize and encourage construction sites managed in an environmentally and socially considerate and accountable manner.
Environmental issue	Construction site impacts
Objective	To recognize and encourage construction sites managed in a manner that mitigates environmental impacts.
Environmental issue	Security
Objective	To encourage the design of developments where people feel safe and secure; where crime and disorder, or the fear of crime, does not undermine quality of life or community cohesion.

Design Category	**Surface Water Run-off**
Environmental issue	Management of surface water run-off from developments (mandatory)
Objective	To design housing developments that avoid, reduce and delay the discharge of rainfall to public sewers and watercourses. This will protect watercourses and reduce the risk of localized flooding, pollution and other environmental damage.
Environmental issue	Flood risk
Objective	To encourage housing development in low flood risk areas, or to take measures to reduce the impact of flooding on houses built in areas with a medium or high risk of flooding.

A green roof will help reduce surface water run-off from the roof.

Design Category	**Ecology**
Environmental issue	Ecological value of site
Objective	To encourage development on land that already has a limited value to wildlife, and discourage the development of ecologically valuable sites.
Environmental issue	Ecological enhancement
Objective	To enhance the ecological value of a site.
Environmental issue	Protection of ecological features
Objective	To protect existing ecological features from substantial damage during the clearing of the site and the completion of construction works.
Environmental issue	Change in ecological value of site
Objective	To reward steps taken to minimize reductions and to encourage an improvement in ecological value.
Environmental issue	Building footprint
Objective	To promote the most efficient use of a building's footprint by ensuring that land and material use is optimized across the development.
Design Category	**Waste**
Environmental issue	To recognize and reward the provision of adequate indoor and outdoor storage space for recyclable and non-recyclable household waste.
Objective	Storage of non-recyclable waste and recyclable household waste (mandatory).
Environmental issue	Construction waste management (mandatory)
Objective	To promote reduction and effective management of construction-related waste by improving on performance which meets the Site Waste Management Plan (SWMP) Regulations.
Environmental issue	Composting
Objective	To encourage developers to provide the facilities to compost household waste, reducing the amount of household waste sent to landfill.

you even purchase your site as it will inform you about how suitable a prospective site is for achieving a truly sustainable home. It goes without saying that you will also want to gather as much information as possible about sustainable issues that are likely to have an impact on the way in which you build your house.

The Planning Stage

Setting the Brief

Having gathered all of this information, the next step is to analyse it with regard to what it is exactly you want the house to do for you, and from this formu-

Site for sale with sign board.

late a written brief that tells the designer (even if this is yourself) what your user requirements are. It is also important to commit to what it is that you want the site to do at this stage too, so a thorough site analysis should be undertaken. Important issues that will arise now, and terms that you should become familiar with, include design for energy efficiency and passive solar design. You will no doubt consider the incorporation of renewable energy technologies and make sure that the materials that are to be used for the building fabric are sustainable. In fact you need to decide the degree of sustainability that you wish to achieve and to this end you may wish to refer to some recognized measure of sustainability such as The Code for Sustainable Homes. Before you begin to design you need to decide on what kind of sustainable house you are going to build. You should have some idea of what your overall budget is, and some idea of the overall timescales involved. If you have lots of building experience you will probably be more accurate with your predictions than someone who has not so much experience. Regardless of how much experience you have, you probably need to revise some aspect of your budget, brief or programme as the project develops. The important thing is to plan, then revise your plan, then revise your plan again if necessary, but always work to your plan.

The Design Stage

Outline Design

The third stage is the design stage where the scheme is designed in a schematic way that illustrates that the house and the site are going to do what you want them to do. Then you will need to carry out or commission a preliminary cost estimate for the overall project to see if you can afford to finance the project. To do this you will need to have some knowledge at a very early stage of just how much everything is going to cost, including the cost of the site and associated professional fees, design fees, application fees, and construction costs regardless of which procurement route you choose to follow. Armed with all of the above knowledge you are then in a position to purchase your site knowing that you can build a truly sustainable house. If the project needs to be changed then the third stage is repeated until a satisfactory solution is arrived at. This stage can take quite a few iterations, particularly if you are not quite sure about what it is that you want. If you are employing an architect then you should ask them to help you formulate your brief and agree this at an early stage. Sometimes the brief has to change, but often this decision can only be arrived at after a design has been produced and you have analysed the implications of your design brief. Once, and only once, you have arrived at a satisfactory design that is within your budget you should proceed to the next step. Health and Safety issues should already have begun to be considered by this stage, as it is a requirement for designers and clients to do so.

Detailed Design

The next step is to develop the design and site layout and prepare a detailed cost estimate, and if everything is still achievable, then apply for planning consent. This step can take a considerable length of time and can be frustrating if you are itching to get building, but it is important that you do not build anything until you have obtained planning consent, just in case the planners insist that a change be made to the form, materials or location of the house on the site. If you are fairly confident that planning consent will be given it may be prudent to begin the working drawings that become the backbone of the production information package. Generally speaking though, it is wise to wait until planning consent is granted before starting working drawings just in case there is some requirement imposed by the planners that would result in abortive drawing work and associated fees from your design team. A detailed design cost check should be made to ensure that everything is still within budget.

Working Drawings

Following planning consent being awarded, the working drawings and a detailed specification for the project can be finalized. Having obtained planning consent it is important that the overall size or height of the house is not changed, nor is the external appearance, as this will mean that you will have to reapply for planning consent all over again with subsequent delays in your overall programme. Some minor changes may be made, provided that the local planning authority consider these to be de minimis. Having working drawings to hand and a detailed specification will allow the project to be priced to a much greater degree of accuracy.

Building Control

Once your working drawings have been completed, a Building Control application can be made. As soon as you have lodged your drawings with building control you can start work on site, provided that you send them the requisite notices and give them sufficient warning to organize site inspection visits. If your house design and proposed method of construction is considerably different from normal modes of construction, and your Building Control Officer is unsure as to whether it will comply, it will be your responsibility to prove that the design meets the requirements of the regulations. In such a case you should probably agree each stage of construction with building control before you begin.

Tendering and Letting the Contract

The working drawings and specifications are developed to a stage where everything has been detailed and described to a sufficient level to allow for full pricing and tendering the project. They should allow full bills of quantities to be produced if you are following a traditional procurement route, or full lists of materials if you are taking a more hands-on approach. Contractors and sub-contractors should also be approached at this stage to gauge their interest in tendering for the job. You should decide on the form of tender and contract to be used and if you are using a contractor, let him know from the outset that you are building a sustainable house.

The Construction Stage

Health and Safety

Operations on site should begin with securing the site boundaries to prevent unauthorized entry and posting such notices warning that hard hats and other appropriate safety gear should be worn at all times. This is now a requirement under Health and Safety regulations for all contractors, and is good practice for the self-builder as it keeps health and safety uppermost in everyone's mind – particularly those who may have cause to enter the site. Remember that building sites are dangerous places. Before embarking on any piece of work it is worth noting down just what that work will entail, how you are going to go about it, and what risk may be associated with that particular work item. This should raise your awareness of all the associated risks and allow you to plan and implement safety measures firstly to eliminate the risk, or at least to mitigate the risk and reduce it to an acceptable level. Do not let anyone on the site who is not prepared to wear appropriate personal protection equipment (PPE) and be prepared to remove anyone from the site who fails to comply with any reasonable health and safety instruction. One final note of warning: always use appropriate means of access, including scaffolding, as the work progresses in order to help prevent accidents.

The Building Process

There are many stages in the building process, ranging from protecting existing ecological features to clearing the site area where your house is to be located, through substructure to superstructure to finishing out and decorating. At every stage you should minimize the environmental impact of the building process itself by utilizing local contractors and labour and using local materials and suppliers. You should endeavour to operate your site in a way consistent with the 'considerate constructors' scheme' so that you minimize discomfort to your neighbours during the building process. You should also minimize the amount of waste that leaves the site, and make sure that any waste that must leave the site is segregated into different bins to allow for ease of recycling.

Periodic inspections by building control and whoever is certifying the various stages of construction will be required during this stage.

Health and safety is of paramount concern on every building site (photograph © Keith Lockhart).

Operations off site

While work is progressing on site there is a need to keep up to date with other work associated with the building process, but which does not necessarily require you to be on site to do it. You will need to keep your paperwork up to date, including keeping all of your receipts for claiming back VAT if the materials have not been zero-rated at source. You will need to price around for materials to get the best deals to keep the cost to a minimum. You will also need to scrutinize invoices for work carried out by others to ensure that they are paid only for work carried out. Do not make any up-front payments for work to be carried out, but do be sure to make your payments on time. Only withhold payments for poor workmanship if it has previously been agreed in writing that it is acceptable for you to do so.

The Commissioning Stage

During this stage you or the specialists you have employed should carry out a comprehensive commissioning programme to ensure that everything works as it should. This will include all ventilation, electrical, and plumbing installations.

Commissioning of specialist equipment should be carried out by specialists.

Completion

It is a very satisfying feeling to move into a house that you have constructed yourself or had a hand in building. There is, however, the temptation to move into the house before it is completely finished. There may be a number of perfectly good reasons for moving in early but if you can possibly avoid this then do. With the best will in the world, you will not make the same progress on your house once you have moved in as you would have if you had simply finished it off before moving. Two common reasons for moving in early are running out of time and running out of money. It is not a good enough reason that you have run out of money; you probably did not budget properly. It is not a good enough reason that you have run out of time; you probably did not have a realistic programme. These two pitfalls can be avoided with good project management, careful budgeting and careful programming.

The Sustainable Home Checklist

- Have you/will you address energy efficiency and CO_2 emissions?
- Have you/will you address pollution arising from the manufacture and use of products built into your home?
- Have you/will you address water use internally and externally?
- Have you/will you address health and wellbeing issues in your new home?
- Have you/will you use only sustainable materials and materials that are certified as being responsibly sourced?
- Have you/will you address issues of management including construction site impacts and provide building user guides so that others can optimize the performance of the systems in the house?
- Have you/will you design to minimize the impact of surface water run-off?
- Have you/will you seek to improve the overall ecological value of your site?
- Have you/will you minimize waste generated during the construction process and minimize and manage household waste?

CONCLUSION

This chapter has stated the moral imperative for building in a sustainable way. It has outlined a method of measuring just how sustainable your house could be and raised the issues that must be considered at an early stage in the process. It has then outlined the tasks that need to be carried out when building your own house. Of necessity, not every detail has been covered, simply enough to make you aware of the extent of the task.

If it all seems too overwhelming, you need to remember that what you are doing is simply a single project with a number of distinct phases and a list of sub-projects. The way to ensure that everything goes as smoothly as possible is to manage the project in a coordinated way in order to achieve the best possible outcome. Chapter Two provides further information on how to manage the whole process from start to finish. One of the fundamental questions it asks you to ask yourself is 'am I going to do this task myself, or am I going to get someone else do it for me?' This book is written to allow you to make an informed decision either way.

Project Management

This chapter looks at the importance of managing the whole project from inception to completion. It emphasizes the importance of treating every stage of the planning, design and building process as separate but interrelated projects in their own right. Someone must manage each of these projects; either this is carried out by the self-builder or by someone else. It identifies the skills required to accomplish each project and asks the question time and again: 'if I cannot do this then who will and what will it cost?' Some basic guidelines and checklists are given for managing each stage of the overall project.

When you are building your own house you become a project manager. The extent of your role will depend on how much you want to get involved in the overall process and on the time that you can devote to the project. The importance of this role cannot be emphasized enough. Remember that project management is for some people a full time job, so do not underestimate the time commitment required for this role. Remember too, that your role and involvement may vary from stage to stage. What you should try to do is work to your strengths, and then employ others to do those tasks that you do not want to tackle.

Some basic project management terminology may be useful at this point so let's begin with the definition of a project. A project is usually defined as a group of interrelated work activities that are constrained by a specific scope, budget and programme to deliver the stated goal.

The key components of project management are: that every project has a beginning and an end, and every project is defined by its scope, budget and programme. Also, from a project management perspective, the phases in the life of a house-building project are initiation, planning, design, construction, commissioning, and completion.

In building a house for yourself, the overall project is the construction of the house. To do this you will engage in many different work activities, each of which must be treated as projects in their own right. Think of them as mini-projects. It is important to realize that many of these mini-projects will be running simultaneously, particularly during the construction phase, so organization is the key. The level of your involvement in each of these mini-projects will obviously depend on the phase and how your skill levels match up to the tasks associated with that phase.

PROJECT MANAGEMENT WITH MINIMUM INVOLVEMENT

Every stage of the design and building process requires to be managed. Let's say, for the sake of argument, that you have decided to do the minimum amount of work on your self-build and, instead of trying to tackle everything yourself, you are going to employ people to manage the project for you. Even if this is the case there is a role for you to play as the project owner. You will have to decide on which experts you will employ to carry out the various tasks that need to be completed. Traditionally you would employ an architect as the person to coordinate the design process. Do not choose the architect at random, however, as architects come in all shapes and sizes. The relevant professional body in your area (RIBA in England and Wales, RIAS in Scotland, RSUA in Northern Ireland and RIAI in Southern Ireland) will be able to put you in touch with architects with the right kind of experience. Check that they have sustainable credentials at the very least. Ask to see examples of their work on similar projects to yours and ask them to elaborate on the extent of the service that they normally provide and ensure that you agree fees early in the process. Since the architect is the person who has overall responsibility for the design process, then they are in the best position to inform you who else may be required on the design team and the extent of the services required from them. At the very minimum, you will require the services of a quantity surveyor to provide cost advice, and very possibly the services of a structural engineer if the house is anything other than standard construction. You may wish to employ the services of a CDM coordinator to provide advice and maintain health and safety standards to ensure that the design complies with the Construction Design Management Regulations (see the section following on the CDM Regulations). You will need to inform the design team of your requirements and provide the design team with a brief. You will have to communicate with the architect and others in the design team to keep informed of progress throughout the design and build phases of the project. You will need to agree the overall budget including design fees. You will need to agree target dates for and sign off on completion of the various stages. The most important aspect of your role is the ability to make decisions and timely ones at that.

In a situation where you wish to have minimum involvement in the construction stage then a traditional procurement route may be the best course of action for your project. However, in any event you should take advice from your design team, as there are a number of procurement routes available to you. The traditional route involves a package of information being prepared by the design team to a sufficient level to allow a main contractor to price the building aspect of the work within the conditions imposed by the chosen contract. The tender package should include a description of the main conditions of contract to be used including: the duration of the contract; detailed construction drawings; a bill of quantities (BOQ) or, if the project is too small to warrant a full BOQ, then at the very least a schedule of work/rates/materials and any other information that may be relevant to the building of your house. There are a number of standard building contracts that are tried and tested so there is no point in trying to reinvent the wheel. Take advice from your design team and choose the type of contract that best meets your needs. If you follow the traditional procurement route of appointing a main contractor, then in this instance the main contractor will be the one who coordinates all of the on-site operations including the appointment and coordination of all of the sub-contractors. Normally it is the architect who administers the contract on your behalf. The contract is the agreement between you and the contractor, which specifies what work has to be carried out, when it has to be completed, and what happens if it is not completed in a timely or satisfactory manner. Furthermore it contains clauses relating to your responsibilities as an employer and in particular your responsibility to pay the contractor for work carried out. Contracts of this nature have been developed over a great many years and are designed to protect each party to the contract in the event of default by either party. If everything goes according to plan, then at the end of the contract period you will have the house that you wanted, all of the bills will have been paid, and all of the statutory undertakings will have been met. The final stages of the contract include handover of the finished building and any site-works included in the contract. It is important to ensure that the building is finished before handover, but if it isn't then it is important to identify which parts are finished and which parts remain unfinished and that you only take possession of those parts that are finished. In such a case a notice of partial possession/completion should be issued by the architect in order to clearly identify those works which are being taken over. There will normally be a defects period where the contractor is responsible for making good any latent defects that appear after the house has been certified as being practically complete.

So you can see that even in circumstances where you wish to have minimum involvement, you still have significant roles to play.

TYPICAL ROLES AND RESPONSIBILITIES

There are so many things to think about, so many tasks to be undertaken, and so much specialist knowledge required, that you may be questioning the whole idea of building your own sustainable and energy efficient house. If the whole thing just looks like a mine-field then just remember that you do not have to do everything yourself. There are many specialists available who can be called upon to do their bit in making your dream a reality. The following section outlines those who would normally be responsible for carrying out particular tasks and, should you wish not to tackle these yourself, you should allocate those tasks to the relevant specialist. On some difficult sites the number of specialists that need to be engaged can be frightening, so make sure you or your architect carry out a good feasibility study before rushing out and buying any old piece of land. Architects tend to work to a clearly defined work plan known as the RIBA *Plan of Work* so it is

worthwhile outlining their terminology so that it is clear what their tasks will be if appointed. The 2007 version of the *Plan of Work* is broken down into five phases which, taken together, contain eleven stages. You can appoint an architect for any or all of the eleven RIBA stages. The eleven stages have been integrated into our five project management stages below. Some of the stages may overlap, and on occasion the order may change somewhat depending on the nature and complexity of the project.

Initiation stage

Client

You as the client begin the process, it's your project and you can do as much or as little as you wish.

Architect

If you have your eye on a site you may wish to appoint an architect to investigate it and carry out a feasibility study to see just what kind of sustainable home you will be allowed to build. The first phase of the RIBA plan of work is called the Preparation Phase and it contains stages A and B. Stage A is the appraisal stage and this includes: the architect investigating the client's objectives and possible constraints on development; the preparation of feasibility

Finding your ideal site can be a challenge.

studies; and an assessment of options to enable the client to decide whether to proceed. Stage B is the design brief stage, which fits into our planning stage below.

Solicitor

If you decide that you wish to purchase the site then you will want to appoint a solicitor to carry out such things as title searches and to complete the purchase for you.

Bank or Building Society

If you need to borrow money to purchase the site or to carry out the construction stage then now is the time to get an agreement with your lender to allow you to proceed.

Valuer

You may be required to get an independent valuation carried out on the value of the site and potential value with the proposed dwelling before the lending authority will agree to a loan.

Project Planning Stage

Client

During this stage you will make a number of decisions regarding the overall size and location of your house and also which consultants you are going to use, if any. You will also develop the design brief that will include a programme of all the spaces that are required along with a general description of what it is that you want the house to be like. You should also establish your budget and, if you are employing consultants, then inform them of your budget at an early stage. Your consultants should then be in a position to work to your budget and tell you approximately what you can achieve for your budget. All too often however expectations exceed budget and will require that you either lower your expectations or raise your budget.

Design Consultants

If you are going to employ consultants to carry out the design to your requirements, then it is often good practice to appoint a lead consultant who will organize the rest of the consultants on your behalf. This role has traditionally been the remit of the archi-

tect, but there are other consultants who can carry out this role equally well. The architect normally has the greatest input into a project, however, and is often involved from the inception through to completion, and has a reasonable grasp of the input required from all of the other consultants. Money spent on good design is money well spent, particularly if you end up with a house that exceeds your expectations. Make sure that your consultants have experience of sustainable design. The RIBA Stage B is the design brief stage, which includes the development of the initial statement of requirements into the design brief and confirms the key requirements and possible constraints. It also includes the identification of relevant procurement methods and procedures and the range of consultants that are required to be engaged on the project.

Design Stage

Client

If you can read and produce drawings and coordinate spatial relationships, then you may well be in a position to design your own home. Bear in mind however, that architectural design is a specialist vocation that takes years of study and practice to qualify for professional recognition. If you do employ an architect then your role is to initiate the design stage and review the designs created by the architect to ensure that they conform fully to your requirements. Use the checklists in this book to help you formulate the brief and to check that your requirements have been incorporated into the design.

Architect

Most architects in the UK and Ireland work to a standard plan of work such as that produced by the Royal Institute of British Architects (RIBA). The RIBA Plan of Work Design Phase consists of Stages C, D and E. Stage C is the concept stage where the concept design is developed and additional relevant information is prepared. The concept will include: outline proposals for the structure and building services elements; an outline specification; a preliminary cost plan; and a review of the procurement route.

Stage D, design development, develops the concept design and includes the development of the structural and building services systems and the

Sketch design 3D drawing.

outline specification and the cost plan. By this stage the project brief should be finalized and the scheme design fixed. The planning application is normally made at the end of RIBA Stage D. Stage E, technical design, begins the preparation of the technical design and specifications and the coordination of components and elements that will contribute to the building control application and applications for any other statutory approvals that may be required.

Quantity Surveyor

If you are employing a quantity surveyor (QS) to advise you on cost matters, they will be able to produce a budget cost estimate based on the outline design drawings and outline specification. If the cost estimate is within your budget you will then be in an informed position to approve the design. If, however, the budget cost estimate is too high, you can request an amendment to the design proposals to bring them in line with your budget. If you are going down the route of having a main contractor do the building work, then the quantity surveyor should prepare bills of quantities to allow for full pricing by the contractor.

Allow space for service runs.

Mechanical and Electrical Engineer

If the project is large enough to warrant the services of mechanical and electrical engineers, then they will produce an outline design of the building services to allow preparation of the budget cost for these elements of the project. It is important that the architect coordinate the overall design of these elements so that there are no surprises when it comes to the detailed design stage.

Structural Engineer

At the outline design stage the structural engineer will provide advice on non-typical structural elements such as foundation systems for difficult ground conditions. This information will then form part of the overall design considerations and inform the budget cost estimate. Drawings and calculations that are required for statutory approvals should be completed and incorporated in the construction drawings.

Planner

If the application is likely to be contentious when it is submitted to planning, and you or your architect are not confident about the approach that should be taken, then you may need the services of a planning consultant. They will produce a planning report that will be submitted to the planning authority along with the drawings and application forms. The planning report will discuss how the proposals conform to the relevant planning policies and present a structured argument for approval.

Roads Consultant

If there are likely to be difficulties with site access, or if there are any other road difficulties, a traffic engineer may need to produce a report to accompany the planning application.

Ecology Consultant

If there is the possibility of endangered plant or animal species such as bats or newts being present on your site, then you may need the services of an ecologist to provide a report to show how they will be protected. You may also need the services of an ecologist if you plan to build on contaminated land.

Archaeologist

Where your site is close to areas of known archaeological interest, then the services of a qualified archaeologist may be required to excavate test trenches or keep a watching brief on site excavations as they occur.

As you can see, if the need arises, there is a wide range of specialist professionals who may be consulted at the design stage. For the architect working to the RIBA plan of work the pre-construction phase follows hard on the heels of the design stage. It consists of stages F, G and H. Stage F sees the preparation of production information to a stage where tenders can be invited and where the building control application can be submitted along with further information gathered and prepared for construction purposes. Stage G, tender documentation, is the preparation of the tender documentation to be issued for tender purposes. Stage H, tender action, identifies and evaluates potential contractors and any specialists that may be required, obtains the tenders and appraises them, and submits recommendations to the client.

The Construction Stage

Client

If a contractor is to be appointed then you will be required to sign the formal contract between you and the contractor. There are a number of standard forms of building contract that can be used. Take advice from your architect or quantity surveyor in relation to the most appropriate form to be used. If you are employing a main contractor or sub-contractors directly then you will need to take out your own employers' insurance and public liability insurance. Check also that any contractors you employ have valid insurance in place. Check both cover and renewal dates. Remember that under a standard contract you are the employer. You are responsible for honouring certificates of payment in full and within the period specified in the contract. If you have employed an architect to administer the contract on your behalf, remember that it is only the architect who can issue empowered instructions to the contractor. This does not mean that you cannot change your mind about something on site, but it does ensure that any changes, whether they be omissions or additions, are treated in a fair and equitable manner and are incorporated into the contract by way of architect instructions. You will be required to attend regular progress and/or technical meetings to hear progress reports from each party involved and discuss the implications of any technical queries from the client perspective.

Architect

The construction phase of the RIBA Plan of Work consists of Stage J, mobilization and Stage K, construction to practical completion. Stage J consists of letting the contract, appointing the contractor, issuing information to the contractor, checking that insurances are in place and arranging the site handover. Stage K is the administration of the building contract through to practical completion, periodically inspecting the site to ensure that the works are generally in accordance with the contract documentation, providing the contractor with further information as and when required, and the reviewing of information provided by the contractor and specialists for compliance with the contract. It is the architect's responsibility to advise you of any additional costs, fees or amendments to the agreed programme.

Contractor

If a main contractor has been appointed then they will take possession of the site and assume responsibility for site safety. It is the contractor's responsibility to carry out the works described in the contract documents in a timely manner and with due diligence. It is also the contractor's responsibility to comply with empowered instructions. A programme of work should be prepared by the contractor which should be agreed by the client. This programme should highlight where additional information is required and where further decisions need to be made and when any persons directly employed by the client are programmed to start and finish. The contract should set out the conditions and terms of payment and the contractor should claim only for work carried out to a satisfactory standard and for which certificates of payment have been issued.

Sub-contractors

Like the main contractor, sub-contractors are also obliged to carry out their work in a diligent and timely manner. It goes without saying that any sub-contractors that you employ directly should be prepared to sign a contract between you as employer and them as sub-contractor. Remember that if one sub-contractor lets you down, this may affect the programme of other contractors and may lead to claims for loss and expense.

Quantity Surveyor

If you have employed a quantity surveyor to look after costs for you, then they will carry out valuations on the amount of work completed and agree payments due to the contractor. Agreed figures will be issued to the architect who will then issue interim payment certificates to you the employer.

Structural Engineer

During the construction stage the structural engineer will make periodic checks to ensure that the main structural elements are being constructed to the required standards.

Mechanical and Electrical Engineer

If you have employed mechanical and electrical engineers then they too will make periodic inspections of the work and report on progress as required. If variations are required, then these will be forwarded to the architect for the issue of an Architect's Instruction.

Building Control

During the construction stage the local building control officer will visit the site to ensure that the construction is generally being constructed in a manner that complies with the building control regulations. There are a number of key inspections where the contractor is required to give notice to building control to allow them to inspect the work. Your local building control office will give you an information pack containing the requisite notices.

Commissioning Stage

Client

It is important that you do not take possession of any

of the services until they have been fully commissioned by the relevant parties and signed off as appropriate.

Main Contractor and Sub-contractors

It is normally the main contractor who is responsible for commissioning the electrical and mechanical services within a house, but the work is carried out and certified by the electrical subcontractor, gas fitters and plumbers as appropriate.

Architect

If you are employing an architect then the architect should ensure that all systems are fully commissioned and operational as expected before signing the certificate of practical completion. Snagging lists should be prepared and any defective workmanship made good before the certificate of practical completion is signed.

Mechanical and Electrical Engineers

If the building services are complicated or you are not prepared to leave the design of the services to the plumber or electrician then you will probably need to employ mechanical and electrical engineers. In this instance it will be the mechanical and electrical engineers who will ensure that the systems within the house are commissioned correctly.

Completion Stage

Client

If you have employed a main contractor to carry out the work and the contract has been fulfilled in relation to progress and quality, then at the stage of practical possession you will take possession of the completed building from the contractor. At this stage half of any retention money is released to the contractor and if there is a clause in the contract for liquated damages then the contractor's responsibility for this ends. Normally there is a defect's liability period built into the contract where the contractor is responsible for rectifying any defects that may arise during this period. Once the defect's liability period has passed and the contractor has made good any defects, all retention monies must be released upon issue of the Final Certificate. The issue of the final certificate brings the terms of the building contract to a close.

Architect

The Use Phase of the RIBA *Plan of Work* consists of Stage L, post practical completion. During this stage the architect will administer the building contract after practical completion and will make final inspections. Assistance will be given to the building user during the initial occupation period and a review of the building in use will be carried out. The architect will issue the Final Certificate at the end of the defect's liability period once the defects have been made good.

Quantity Surveyor

The quantity surveyor will complete a final valuation and ensure that only monies due to the contractor are included in the final certificate. Full account will be taken of any variations that have arisen during the contract.

Contractor

It is the contractor's duty to hand over the completed building on the issue of the Certificate of Practical Completion. The contractor must also make good any defects that arise within the defect's liability period and in a timely manner.

Building Control

Once your house is completed Building Control will make a final inspection and certify the building as being in general accordance with the building regulations.

DOING IT ALL YOURSELF

If you decide to do everything, or almost everything, yourself then you need to be even more organized than those using the traditional procurement method of appointing a full design team and employing a main contractor. In these circumstances the most important role that you will undertake is the role of project manager. Remember that you can always appoint someone else to do specific tasks.

Initiation Stage

Every project begins with initiation of the overall planning of the project and should include environmental aspects and funding and the initial concept design. You will no doubt have noticed that the phases of initiation, planning and design overlap to some extent but what is important is that each of the phases, and each work activity within each phase, is treated as a mini-project with a beginning and an end, and a scope, a budget and a programme.

During project initiation you need to plan what the project is and how it is to be implemented. Most importantly, write it down. This written documentation will form the Project Requirement Document, will establish the project organizational structure and form the basis for the project management plan. The Project Requirement Document is simply a description of your overall goal. This may be as simple as stating the goal of this project is to design and build as sustainable a house as possible for under £250,000. You may be asking the question: why write it down? The simple answer is that in order to work efficiently, you need to plan, and in order to plan efficiently you need to commit to your plan in writing. Programmes and budgets have a natural tendency to slip, so by committing your plan to writing, you will at the very least have a record of how far things have actually slipped. The goal, however, is not to let anything slip, so a written plan is the best method of ensuring that everything is included and that you stick to the programme targets.

You now need to make some difficult decisions about what exactly you are going to do on the project and what you are going to allow others to do. As the scope of the project unfolds these decisions may become a little easier to make. Remember that very few people are experts in everything. Sometimes it is better to relinquish control of some aspect to an expert who will do a better job than you ever will do. Do not be afraid to change your mind on your role as the project unfolds. Already you have begun the planning stage.

Planning Stage

In order to formulate your brief you will need to ask yourself the question: what is it that I really want from my house? When you are doing this try to describe the qualitative aspects of the house and leave the quantitative aspects to later. For example, you may wish the house to be comfortable all year round.

You may want the house to be full of natural light and take full advantage of free heat gains from the sun. You may want to minimize your reliance on conventional sources of energy. You may want to use only sustainable materials and minimize the amount of wastage on site. You may allow some materials that are less sustainable than others for financial reasons. You may wish to minimize the size of the house you are going to build as this has the largest influence on the overall environmental impact; however, for one reason or another most people want the largest house they can possibly afford. The urge to build a large house may be due to high expectations on the standard of accommodation that you require or may have to do with getting a reasonable return on the high cost of building land in the British Isles. Whatever your reason, it is worth questioning your lifestyle to see if you can make it more sustainable and in the process reduce the size of house you propose. You may want your house to be located in a town close to services and amenities and transport hubs, or in a village in the countryside or even located remotely and isolated from contact with the outside world. You may want your house to be introverted, or extroverted. You may want the whole process to be completed within a particular period of time or by a significant date. You may already know what your budget is, but if you don't, then now is the time to establish exactly how much you are willing and able to spend. As you begin to write your goals you may find that some begin to conflict with others. If this is the case you may have to prioritize your goals and decide which ones are achievable and which are to be sacrificed in order to achieve the overall goal of building your own sustainable house. These project goals will inform every other decision that you will make throughout the project so serious consideration should be given to them. Only you can make these decisions, but you may wish to take advice from others who have more experience in the different aspects under consideration.

That takes care of the house and its location; now ask yourself: what approach am I going to take to manage and carry out the work to implement the project and in particular, how much of the project am I going to tackle myself? Then ask yourself: if I do not do it then who will; what are their responsibilities; and what form will the project organizational structure take? One final aspect that must not be overlooked is: when is all of this work going to be done? Write down your preliminary timetable or programme for each aspect of the work above, adjusting the overall programme to suit sub-project programmes and ensuring that the critical path can be achieved.

Design

Self Design

It is always best to employ someone with experience of the particular task that is being asked of them. If you are going to tackle the design yourself, then I am going to assume that you have all of the necessary skills to design and am not going to tell you how to go about it in this book.

A sustainable timber house building kit from a specialist company.

House Plan Books

If you are going to choose your house design from a book of house plans and have the drawings prepared by a technician, then you will likely end up with a very standard house in every way, which may be very cheap and very buildable but will neither be particularly energy efficient nor sustainable. Until such times as house plan books are updated to include sustainable solutions they should be avoided unless there is a plan which meets all of the requirements of your brief and can be achieved as a sustainable solution.

Specialist Firms

There are a number of firms that specialize in sustainable technologies who are quite capable of providing good advice and some go as far as preparing designs for you or will take your own plans and develop them into a more sustainable solution. Beware however of companies that provide only one solution which happens to be the one for which they hold the franchise. You may not get the most sustainable house for your proposed budget.

Design Consultants

Consultant services include but are not limited to: architect, civil engineer, structural engineer, geotechnical engineer, environmental engineer, surveyor, traffic engineer, noise consultant, landscape architect, utilities coordinator, planner, financial consultant, construction manager, cost estimator, scheduler, and testing specialists.

The scope of your project will determine the range of consultants, if any, that you will appoint; but by far the most important consultant is the architect.

During the design phase there are a number of tasks that are undertaken by design consultants. They will help to firm up and establish the design brief based on your requirements and assess and address project risks. The architect will produce a conceptual design and the engineering consultants will produce engineering and technical studies consistent with the principles of sustainable design. The initial proposals should be reviewed from value engineering and risk assessment perspectives. The consultants should be able to estimate the capital cost and running costs of your house, particularly in relation to energy use.

Project management may include organizing plant hire (photograph © Keith Lockhart).

Your consultants will also prepare the planning application to include drawings, outline specification and any additional supplementary information as required by the local planning authorities. Where required they will help develop a construction schedule with each work element clearly identified. Once the entire preliminary and detail design has been agreed, the consultants will prepare final design drawings and specifications and should update cost estimates throughout the design process. Prior to obtaining tenders, they will produce final design and working drawings and specifications for the construction package and update these as required during the construction stage.

Construction

Your role as a project manager during the construction phase will depend to a great degree on whether you are employing a general builder to construct your house, or if you are going to employ subcontractors directly, or even whether you are going to tackle some of the work yourself. There are advantages and disadvantages with whichever route that you choose.

Employing a General Builder

A good general builder, or main contractor if you wish, is worth his weight in gold but is hard to come by. A general builder will organize site safety, sub-contractors, materials ordering and delivery, building inspectors, plant hire, and all the administration behind all of the above activities. To a large extent a general builder is a project manager of the building task. Some builders are better organized than others with the result that they are better at project management. When times are good in the building trade and there is lots of work, the not so good builders will take on too much work and be unable to cope with the additional workload. Many people feel let down by their builder and therefore develop a deep distrust because they have been let down time and time again and this is probably one of the main reasons for people to tackle self-build projects. However, if you take on the role of general builder yourself, you will soon discover how difficult a job it really is. You will be let down by suppliers and sub-contractors alike and this will force you to reconsider the route you are proposing to take or to reconsider the project programme. Before you employ your builder it is well worth running a few simple checks. Ideally, you should choose a builder who has tackled a self-build type of project before, that way they will know and be able to anticipate the pitfalls. It is worth going to have a look at some of the work they have carried out in the past and checking their standard of workmanship. Talk to the clients who employed them and see how easy they are to work with.

Employing Sub-contractors

As with a main contractor, you should run a few preliminary checks to ensure that sub-contractors are capable of carrying out the work. Once again it is worthwhile having a look at some previous jobs that they have worked on to ensure that they are in fact capable. If they are domestic sub-contractors working for the main contractor then it is the main contractor who is responsible for their work.

Commissioning

The ultimate goal of commissioning is to ensure that all of the systems and sub-systems contained in your house are fully operational and optimized from the time you begin to use them. In a sustainable house these systems will probably comprise ventilation, plumbing including solar water heating, electrical,

data and communications, fire and security. As part of the commissioning process, all compliance certificates and system instructions should be collected together and form the basis of the building-user manual. Just as you would expect to be given a user manual if you were to purchase a new car, so too a user manual should be provided with a new house and while you may know every system inside out, not every future building user will have the same intimate knowledge.

Completion

Try to resist the urge to move into your house before everything is complete. If you have worked to your programme and budget there is no reason for having to move into what is still a building site. If you really must move in early then it is vital that you programme the outstanding work to ensure that you actually do complete everything. If you have had to borrow money to build your house, then you will need your architect or other building certifier to certify that the house is complete before the final payment can be released.

THE CDM REGULATIONS

Due to the large number of deaths and serious accidents that happen on building sites, the Governments of the UK and Ireland introduced legislation designed to allow the working practices on building sites to be regulated. In the UK the Construction (Design and Management) Regulations 1994 (CDM Regulations) came into effect in 1994 and were subsequently amended in 2007. Their aim is to reduce the occurrence of accidents and occupational ill-health arising from construction work. To do this the key objective of the Regulations is to ensure that construction health and safety risks are avoided, mitigated or managed and that your construction project is safe to build, use and maintain. Those three words, 'avoid, mitigate and manage' are in order of importance and are the key considerations.

There are four main types of accident that cause death on building sites and these should be given the utmost consideration. These comprise damage caused by: falls from a height; falling or collapsing trenches or materials; site vehicles; and contact with overhead or underground electricity cables.

Non-fatal injuries that should be guarded against include damage caused by: manual handling; slips, trips and falls on the level; material collapse and falls from heights. In order to prevent this, particular attention should be paid to temporary working platforms, ladders and scaffolds.

From a legal perspective, anyone having construction work carried out has legal obligations under the Construction (Design and Management) Regulations 2007 (CDM 2007) unless they are a domestic client. A domestic client is defined as a person who either lives, or will live, in the building where the work is carried out, provided that the building does not relate to any trade or business or other undertaking. In most instances, those building their own house will fall into the category of domestic client. However, those who are employed by a domestic client to do work on the client's building, for example a main contractor or a sub-contractor or tradesman working on your house, will have duties under CDM 2007; therefore some knowledge of the regulations on the client's part is vital.

As a self-builder you must take the CDM Regulations into account from the very outset of your project, with the overarching consideration 'as far as is reasonably practicable'.

There are two main roles involved. The role of the planning supervisor is the coordination of health and

Welfare facilities include WCs for workers on site (photograph © Keith Lockhart).

safety issues during the project design and planning (CSDS in Ireland). The other main role is that of the Principal Contractor whose main duty is the coordination of health and safety issues during the construction phase of the project (CSPS in Ireland).

Appoint the Right People

For any given task it is important to employ the right people. You can appoint yourself as a CDM coordinator and/or principal contractor if you have the necessary competence and resources to carry out the CDM duties.

Allow Enough Time

Time is a precious resource for everyone. The main responsibility for setting the programme rests with the client. Ensure that enough time is given to any CDM duty holders to allow them to identify and consider potential risks and hazards. The same can be said regarding building contractors: give them enough time to assess potential risks and hazards and carry out their work in a safe and timely manner

Provide Information

Under CDM 2007 the client has to provide information about the site and its immediate surroundings. Failure to do so could result in lengthy delays if work has to stop while risk assessments are carried out. This information should identify any potential risks such as contaminated land or the presence of asbestos.

Communicate and Coordinate

Communication is vital. Everyone working on your site should know all of the risks involved and they are all responsible for ensuring that work is carried out in a safe manner.

Manage

Health and safety actions do not happen in isolation, and like every other aspect of construction, they need to be managed. Ensure that they form part of the agenda of every meeting and make sure that there is a project-specific health and safety file that is kept up to date.

Ensure there are Adequate Welfare Facilities on Site

If you are employing a sub-contractor it is your responsibility to ensure that there are welfare facilities on site. These include toilets and an area to eat lunch.

Further information can be found on the Construction (Design and Management) Regulations 2007, section on the Health and Safety Executive's website (*see* Further Information, page 187).

For the south of Ireland there is a client responsibilities publication which can be viewed on the following website: http://www.hsa.ie/eng/Sectors/Construction/.

Project Management Checklist

- Write project requirements document. (What is the overall goal?)
- Assess your own capability and capacity. (What realistically can I do?)
- Establish project organization structure. (Who is going to do what?)
- Write the programme for the work. (What needs to be done and when?)
- Write supporting programmes. (What needs to be done and when for sub-projects?)
- Quality management. (Who will be responsible for quality management?)
- Risk management. (What are the risks associated with the project and how can these risks be eliminated, minimized or managed, including time, finances, sub-contracts, and physical risks?)
- Contract management. (How will the contract(s) be managed?)

CONCLUSION

Whether you employ others to build your house or do the majority of the work yourself, you have a number of project management roles to fulfil. You can appoint others to carry out the design work, make applications for statutory approvals and invite tenders. Your consultants may administer the building contract on your behalf and check that everything is being built to the required standards, but even at this there is still a significant amount of project management to be carried out by you the client.

Do not take on work that could be better carried out by others, often in less time and with less overall cost. Do appoint the correct consultants who are knowledgeable about sustainable design and construction and who will be able to advise you accordingly. Do appoint contractors who have experience in sustainable construction.

Remember that health and safety does not happen on its own and must be managed as part of the overall project management package.

Above all, treat each and every stage of the design and subsequent building of your house as projects in their own right; projects that require project management. Finally remember that each stage has a beginning and an end and every project is defined by its scope, budget and programme.

CHAPTER THREE

The Site

Chapter Three provides an overview of what to look out for from a sustainability and energy efficiency perspective when considering purchasing a site. It not only covers the ideal site situation where there is good ground to build on, good solar access, good shelter, plenty of room to build and access to roads and public utilities (as most books on the subject do) but it also looks at the less than ideal site (which many self- builders end up building on) and outlines strategies for dealing with the design challenges presented by difficult site conditions. Checklists are given to help analyse the site under investigation.

The best site for your ideal sustainable house will be located in a good neighbourhood where property prices are predictable and where value for money is the order of the day. It will be in an area that is zoned by the planners for housing.

The history of the site will be known and there will be no historical features that will severely restrict the design proposals. There will be no legal complications in connection with the use of the site or disputes and ambiguities with regard to site boundaries. Ground conditions will be such that minimal foundations will be required and there will be no contamination on the site. The topography of the site will lend itself to your proposed site layout and will result in minimal disturbance to natural contours and other ecological features of the site. There will be excellent solar access and the sun will be able to reach all of the windows and proposed outdoor living spaces and in general, the prevailing weather conditions will complement the proposed site layout. There will be opportunities on the site for utilizing other renewable energy resources such as timber plantations or small-scale hydro or wind power. The size of the site will be enough to fit on the proposed house and be in the desired position and will have

sufficient space for all of the other proposed activities. Access to the site will be from the desired direction and will be easily achievable with no disturbance to existing boundary hedges or other natural habitat. All of the public utilities will be available either on or immediately adjacent to the site and the site will be close to rail and bus stops or stations. There will be little or no risk of flooding on or near the site.

If your site meets all of the above criteria then you have all the correct ingredients for a perfect site for a sustainable house, but unfortunately not all sites meet all of the above criteria. Therefore, before you actually purchase your site it is worth carrying out a site analysis to identify its potential for sustainable living. Too often a site analysis is carried out only at the design stage. If you have a choice of sites and you have not yet purchased, then you should use the following steps as a guideline to analyse the site and help you choose the best one. It is worth noting here that site analysis is one of the most important steps in the whole design process, so it should be taken seriously. It not only helps to determine the layout of built form on the site, but also the orientation of the house, the disposition of the major spaces within and

Sometimes the ideal site is on your doorstep (photograph © Keith Lockhart).

around the house, site access and a host of other considerations. By giving due consideration to each of the issues, you will be in a better position to make informed decisions.

SITE ANALYSIS

Site Location

No doubt you have often heard the phrase: 'location, location, location' when it comes to buying or selling property. With sites it is no different. The location of your site is important for three environmental reasons.

Location — Environmental Sustainability

One of the most important factors in the choice of site is its location in relation to household transport requirements. This is because transport is on average the second largest producer of CO_2 per person per annum. For this reason, if you can find a site close to

33

The size of property you build should fit into the grain of the area.

where you work and also where your children will go to school, and close to where most of your socializing will take place, then you will minimize your household's transport related carbon footprint.

A more localized factor is the direct ecological impact of building on a particular site. You should always aim to improve the ecological value of any site and never build in a way that will reduce it.

Location – Economic Sustainability
Given that for most people, the building or purchase of a house is the single largest investment that they will ever make in their lifetime, then for economic reasons alone the choice of a site must be made

wisely. There is little point in building a mansion in an area where the average house prices are low as it will be well nigh impossible for you to recoup your investment should you have to sell up for any reason. Equally, from a purely economic point of view, there is little point in building a very small property in an area where sites are very expensive as once again you will have difficulty in recouping your investment.

Location – Social Sustainability
Social sustainability is that aspect of sustainability which looks at the greater good, and takes society at large, including future generations, into consideration. In terms of choosing a site it will take recogni-

A site in the countryside may seem idyllic but remember your transport carbon footprint.

CONCLUSION

Whether you have carried out the site analysis on your own or had your architect do it for you, you should use it to help you make informed decisions about the layout and design of your house. It is the site analysis that confirms the design as belonging to a particular location, and helps to generate a sense of place and belonging. At the very least, you should use it as an aid to help you review your architect's proposals to ensure that the many issues that have been identified have been considered.

It is worth noting that often there will be a number of conflicting requirements between your brief, the site analysis and the statutory requirements pertaining to the site. A good architect will be able to prioritize these requirements and incorporate them into the initial design proposals, and make it clear why the design has turned out the way it has. Sometimes it is only when the design begins to be realized that you are able to establish your own priorities, and this may lead to revisions in the design proposals. This is all part of the design process.

The site analysis is not only an aid to design. It should be retained, committed to one drawing if possible and submitted as part of the planning application to show the planners the rationale behind some of the design decisions that have been made.

Planning Permission

This chapter gives advice on how and when to approach the planning authorities. It advises discussing the project with the planners at an early stage to avoid abortive work and unnecessary expense.

Planning is the system by which the Government controls what can be built and where it can be built. It has a very important role in society by helping to protect the environment and the amenity value of towns, cities and the countryside. In Chapter Three we mentioned the importance of checking at an early stage whether or not planning consent may possibly be granted for the house you want to construct. So many people have rushed into the design process and designed their ultimate house on their ideal site, only to find that the Planning Authority turns down the planning application and the house they end up with is not the one that they wanted.

It is useful to know how the planning authorities work, and the legislative framework under which they operate, in order to maximize your chances of obtaining the type of planning consent that you want. If you or your consultants possess a high degree of knowledge about the planning system and all of the relevant policies then you can turn planning policy to your advantage when making an application for planning permission for your house. Some of the legislation and policy has more immediate relevance than others.

PLANNING LEGLISATION

Planning policy throughout the UK is currently in a state of flux, and new planning provisions are frequently replacing older policies and guidance notes. It is therefore worth checking with your local planning authority just what policies will be relevant to your application. It is also worth obtaining copies of each of these so that reference can be made to them in your planning application.

Strategic Plans, Regional Plans, Spatial Plans and Regional Spatial Strategies

Regional Development Strategies offer strategic and long-term directions on future development of particular regions for the foreseeable future, often looking ten to twenty years ahead. They tend to be prepared in close consultation with the community and seek to define an agreed vision for particular regions and to frame an agenda which will lead to its successful achievement. They have the effect of influencing the future distribution of activities throughout the particular region and tend not to be limited to land-use planning. Most recognize that policies for physical development have an important bearing on other matters such as the local and regional economy and healthy living environments. Integral to providing strategic and long-term perspectives for development, regional strategies include sustainable development as a specific objective and transport strategies as part of the wider spatial strategy. The development of Regional Plans is one method of

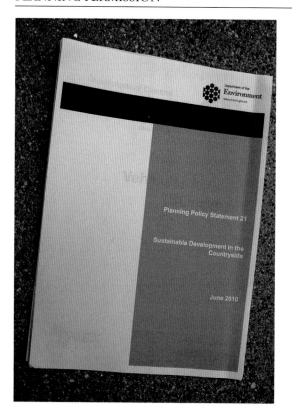

Planning Policy Statement 21 (PPS 21) – Sustainable Development in the Countryside.

Strategy. The aim of development plans in general is to manage development and to ensure that there is enough land available for the expected needs of an area for such things as housing, community facilities and employment. They also have a key role in protecting significant landscape and environmental features. When your local planning authority is considering your planning application the contents of development plans will play an important role in their deliberations. Currently, development plans cover a fifteen-year period but they can be reviewed and amended as necessary during this time.

Development Plans include: Area Plans, Local Plans and Subject Plans. Area Plans cover one or more council areas and currently in Northern Ireland are the main type of Development Plan, but this is likely to change when planning is devolved to local authorities. Local Plans cover a smaller, more clearly defined area, such as a town centre. Subject Plans are used to deal with a particular type of development within a particular area.

Planning Policy Statements

Planning Policy Statements (PPSs) have the most immediate influence on your design and planning application. Planning Policy Statements are procedural policies that set out important aspects of particular topics such as renewable energy, access, movement and parking or the built heritage or may show the policies in place for a particular area of land such as the countryside. All of these policies are taken into account when assessing planning applications.

Supplementary Planning Advice

There are a number of Design Guides, Best Practice Notes, Development Control Advice Notes (DCANs), Conservation Area Guides and so on available from your local planning authority that will provide design guidance as to how you should design for particular localities.

complying with European Union legislation on strategic environmental appraisal.

The important aspect in the above overview is that Regional Development Strategies support sustainable development, so when making a planning application for a sustainable house, ensure that the relevant Regional Development Strategy Document is mentioned in the supporting documentation submitted with your planning application.

Development Plans, Area Plans and Local Development Documents

Development Plans are prepared by the Local Planning Authority in line with the Regional

PRE-PLANNING

Before even beginning to prepare your planning application there are some fundamental checks that you should make at a very early stage that will save time and effort and your budget.

Consultants

Once again, when it comes to your planning application, you need to ask yourself the question: is this a job that I am going to do myself, or am I going to let someone better able do it for me? Regardless of the answer, the best possible planning outcome for you is to be able to build exactly what you want, where you want. If you have little or no knowledge of how the planning system works you may be tempted here to rush off directly to a planning consultant because they give advice on planning issues, but remember, at this stage you do not even have a design. It may be more advisable to seek the services of an architect who has a track record of obtaining good planning outcomes for sustainable dwellings. I say this because while every architect has experience of making planning applications, ideally what you really want is an architect who has the correct experience so that in the long run, their appointment is going to save you time

and money. Not only will they have an appreciation of the planning system, but they will also have an appreciation of what it means to design a sustainable house and the features that may be incorporated.

The first thing to do is to have a look at the Development Plan/Area Plan for the area where the site is located. If you do not have access to a copy go to the local planning authority and ask to have a look at the relevant Area Plan. If possible, have an informal chat with the Planner who is responsible for the area where the site is located, and explain what it is that you are trying to do. If there are fundamental problems with your proposal then now is the correct time to find out. The advice that you receive from the Planning Authority will be offered 'without prejudice' and should be based on the information contained within the relevant Development Plan /Area Plan.

Within the Development Plan are a number of

In conservation areas you may need to replicate features such as these GRP chimneys.

Site for sale with Planning Consent for a replacement dwelling.

maps that show how the planning authorities have zoned the land for the area under consideration. Around settlements you will find a black line drawn that defines the Development Limit of that particular settlement. If your site falls within the development limit then there is a presumption for development, however if your site falls outside the development limit then there is a presumption against development, unless there is another policy that may apply that would permit development on that site.

Other information contained within Development Plan/Area Plan maps includes sites and areas of historical and archaeological interest, designated areas of outstanding natural beauty, areas of town-

scape character, town centre limits, conservation areas and others. If your site falls within any or all of the above, then you will need to take into consideration the relevant information about the planning conditions that apply to the designated zoning. This information can be found within the written component of the Development Plan/Area Plan.

You will need to decide if you are going to apply for outline planning consent or full planning consent. If you or your architect are fairly confident that all of the planning criteria are in your favour, or at least can be construed to be in your favour, and you know exactly what it is that you want to build on the site then you should probably apply for full planning consent. If, however, you want to establish in principle what can be built on the site and what form it has to take, and you are not so confident about whether the proposals will comply with the planning criteria for that area, then you may wish to apply for outline consent in the first instance to obtain a planning decision. An Outline Planning Application is much less onerous than a Full Planning Application in terms of the quantity of information that is required.

MAKING AN OUTLINE PLANNING APPLICATION

A red line around the proposed site on a drawing and a little bit of information on ownership, access and disposal of sewerage and storm water, along with the appropriate forms and fee is often all that is required. If the application is successful you will obtain the outline consent which will include information relating to Reserved Matters. Reserved Matters are stipulations that the planning authority has placed on the proposed development relating to the type and size and location of the development. These may include: the appearance of the dwelling in respect of the way it looks; the means of access including all routes to and within the site, as well as the way these routes link up to other roads and pathways outside the site; the overall site layout which will include all buildings and open spaces within the development, hard and soft landscaping, and the way the buildings and landscaping are laid out in relation to the immediate area outside the site; any requirement for the planting of trees or hedges to screen the dwelling; and the scale of the overall proposed development including information relating the height, width and length of each proposed building. Sites are often purchased with the benefit of outline consent having already been granted for the site.

If your site has outline planning consent then you will need to make a 'Reserved Matters' application within three years of the outline consent being granted (or a lesser period if specified by a condition on the original outline approval). The details of the Reserved Matters application must be in accord with the outline approval and must comply with any conditions attached to the permission.

MAKING AN APPLICATION FOR FULL PLANNING CONSENT

Assuming that you or your architect have carried out the above checks on the Development Plan/Area Plan, and that you have decided to apply for full planning consent, then you should instruct your architect to prepare detailed design drawings for a planning application.

Planning Drawings

Typically the information that is required in drawn form includes: a site location plan drawn at a scale of 1:1250 or 1:2500 with the site outlined in red line and any additional land under the ownership of the applicant outlined in blue and any building to be demolished coloured in green; a survey of the existing site at a scale of 1:500 showing levels, boundaries, buildings, trees and other features on the site; a site layout plan at a scale of 1:500 showing site access, the location of the proposed development and any landscaping works to be included along with proposed ground levels; floor plans, sections and elevations at a scale of 1:100 with external materials indicated on the elevations. It is also useful to submit some three-dimensional images of the proposed dwelling as it can sometimes be difficult to explain the proposals fully in plan, section and elevation only.

Planning Forms

Information required on the planning forms includes names and addresses of the applicants or agents, a succinct description of the proposal, information relating to vehicular and pedestrian access to the site, information on how foul and storm (surface) water is to be disposed of, and information relating to title or ownership.

Planning Report

It is good practice to submit a concise planning report to accompany the application. This should be a summary of all of the relevant planning information that has been given consideration in the application. The following headings will provide a template for such a report and for your convenience the type of information to be provided has been included

A Design Guide for Rural Northern Ireland.

under each of the headings. The purpose behind providing such a report is to let the planners see that you have given due consideration to all of the issues that have a bearing on the decision that they, the planners, have to make. Planning considerations should not be subjective, nor should you give the planners the opportunity to make a subjective decision. Each relevant planning criteria should be addressed and nothing left to chance. You should spell out clearly how the proposed development meets each of the criteria, thus making it more difficult for the planners to use the criteria as an excuse for turning your application down.

Location

As well as providing a drawing with the site outlined in red, it is well worth giving a written description of where the site is located. This may be in the form of a known postal address or with reference to a known postal address, for example 'the site is located at [known postal address]' or, where the site does not yet have a postal address, 'the site is located 100m south-east of [known postal address]'.

Site Boundaries

A description of each of the site boundaries should be given, for example the site is bounded to the north by a post and wire fence with three mature sycamore trees located towards the eastern boundary. The eastern boundary comprises a brick-built wall running the full length of the site. The site is bounded to the south by Windmill Road, and so on.

Planning Context

There are a number of sub-headings that can be covered here. Firstly it is worth stating the principal zoning that the planners have allocated to the site. For example, the site lies wholly within the development limit of 'Settlement Name'. Then if the site has been included within or adjacent to additional policy areas then this too should be acknowledged. For example, 'the site is contained within the area designated "Town Centre Conservation Area" and lies just to the west of the "Local Area" Conservation Area'.

If there are sites of archaeological interest indicated on the Area Plan maps then this too should be acknowledged. Finally list all of the other Planning Policy Statements that are relevant to the application, for example PPS1, PPS21 and so on and any Development Control Advice Notes for example DCAN 15, along with other design advice publications published by the relevant planning authority, for example *Creating Places, A Design Guide for Rural Northern Ireland*, and so on.

Site Topography

Here a description of the general lie of the land should include: any significant topographical features, such as river courses; and the extent, size and direction of any slopes on the site. If the site has a river course on or close to it, or if the site lies within a flood plain, then the planners may insist on a flood risk assessment. If one has already been carried out for the site then include it as supplementary informa-

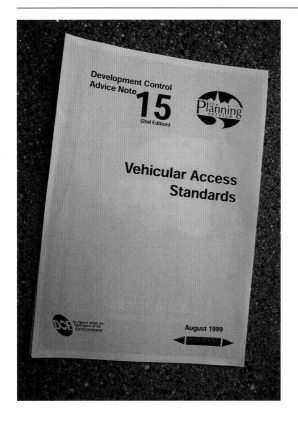

Development Control Advice Note 15 (DCAN 15) – Vehicular Access Standards.

Planning Policy Statement 18 (PPS 18) – Renewable Energy.

tion in the form of an appendix to the planning report. If not, then it is worth checking with the planning authorities (England and Wales) or the local rivers' agency (Northern Ireland) for any published information that is available to the public.

Ground Conditions

Give a brief description of the ground conditions on the site including any areas that are in trees, in grassland or hard-standing. This may be as superficial as 'the ground is generally firm underfoot' or as detailed as you wish to make it.

Site Access and Traffic Considerations

Give a brief description of where access is to be taken from including the road name if appropriate. If you know the speed limit on the section of road where access is to be taken then this will give you an indication of the extent of sight lines that will be required. If sight lines are required then state what the requirements are and how they have been achieved.

Site Context

In this section you should describe the general character of the area in which the site is located. This should include the pattern of land use and the predominant architectural forms and materials that are in use in the surroundings.

Site Analysis

Site analysis is part of the design process and will show the planners all of the influences on the site that have been taken into consideration. This not only should include objective considerations such as potential access locations, a description of where the sun is available on the site, where views are available and so on, but also subjective considerations such as how the site feels and particular sensory considerations.

Design Concept Statement

The design concept statement is not a description of the design. The concept comes before the design and is a statement of what the house is trying to achieve and how it will go about achieving fulfilment of the concept.

Ecological Statement (if Required)

An ecological statement will identify the presence of any ecological features on or near the site and whether or not they need protection.

Archaeology Statement (if Required)

If there are archaeological features on or near the site it may be prudent to employ an archaeologist at an early date to report on the impact of the development on the site and the mitigating measures that need to be taken.

Design Proposals

Provide here a written description of where the site is and what it is that you are proposing for the site. It is good practice to begin with the overall site layout and then move to the house itself, then on to specific details; for example the site is located in the village of Somevillage. Access to the site is from Front Road on the southern boundary of the site. The proposed dwelling is located to the north of the site and comprises a two storey main house with a single storey lean-to return to the front. The house is of modern vernacular design with pitched and slated roofs, smooth white rendered walls, and white painted timber windows and doors. Rainwater goods are black painted aluminium.

Keep the description succinct and objective and refer specifically to how the proposals realize the ideas expressed in the design concept statement. It is here that you will also expand on how the proposals meet the specific criteria contained in the relevant Planning Policy documents. It does no harm to include quotations from these documents to demonstrate how the proposals comply.

Materials

Here you should give a brief summary of the proposed external materials such as roofing materials, wall materials, gutters and down pipes, windows and doors and the colours of each.

Covering Letter

A covering letter should be submitted with the application and should state clearly what is being applied for and should list the documents included in the application.

Planning Report Checklist

- A written description of the site location.
- A written description of the site boundaries.
- A brief acknowledgement of the relevant planning legislation, policies and advice for the site.
- A written description of the topography of the site.
- A brief description of the ground conditions.
- A written description of access to the site and traffic conditions on the road from which access is to be taken.
- A written description of the townscape or rural context of the site including a brief description of the prevalent architecture adjacent to the site.
- A brief written outline of your site analysis.
- A brief written outline of the Design Concept Statement.
- Ecological Statement (if required).
- Archaeology Statement (if required).
- A written description of the design proposals.
- A brief written description of the proposed external materials.

CONCLUSION

The most important aspect of making a planning application is that you know that you are complying with all of the relevant planning policies. There is no point in complying with only nine out of ten policies when the one planning policy that you cannot comply with inevitably leads to a planning refusal. Unless you are very familiar with all of the relevant planning policies, then you are generally better appointing a consultant who will act on your behalf. If you are considering appointing an architect for the design stage, then consider appointing them to prepare the planning application as part of their service. Remember that your architect should have experience in sustainable design. In any event, you or your representative should present as clear a case as possible as to why your application should obtain permission, referring where necessary to the relevant policies. Occasionally the preparation of a planning application will mean having to consult with experts in particular specialist areas such as ecology or archaeology, but remember that this will be money well spent as it will make the planning authority's task easier in granting your Planning Permission.

Purchasing Your Plot

Chapter Five outlines how to go about finding a plot of land, and the legal and contractual obligations involved with purchasing a piece of land (England, Wales, Northern Ireland, Scotland and Southern Ireland).

FINDING YOUR IDEAL SITE

The ideal site is one that you can afford in the right location that is large enough to build your ideal house and is zoned for housing by the planners or already has planning consent. There are a number of ways of going about finding such a site but no one method really stands out above another. Often, those in search of a site will use just whatever methods are available to them at the time.

Magazines
There are a number of self-build publications on the market that list sites for sale across Great Britain and Ireland. In addition, there are property magazines available that concentrate on particular areas and are well worth investigating.

Local Knowledge
One method of finding a site is to use your local knowledge or the local knowledge of someone that you know. The benefit of local knowledge is that you may be able to find a site before it is placed on the open market. If you see a piece of ground or an old house or ruin that may be suitable for a site then it is always worth approaching the owner to enquire if it may be for sale.

It could be that the owner has simply not thought of selling it, perhaps thinking that it does not have much value, so give it a go. To arrive at a fair price, have the potential site valued by a valuer so that you establish a fair market value. The benefit to the vendor is that they can make a sale without all the hassle of advertising, and you get a piece of land without having to worry about being outbid at the last moment. If you have friends who have an eye for site finding, perhaps a builder or other building professional, you may even wish to approach them to see if they know of something that may be suitable for you. When you do spot a plot of land that you like, it is often a good idea to make some local enquiries to find out if there are any other proposed developments in the vicinity of your plot that you have not been made aware of by the vendor.

Estate Agents
Estate agents will usually have a few sites for sale on their books. These will be sites that are on the open market and are subject to market prices. You can just walk into any estate agent and ask to see what they have and you will be treated just like any other member of the public. Do not be tempted to just have a look around at what is on display, but instead try to speak to the most senior person present. Explain to them just what you are looking for and ask them to keep your contact details on record so that

they can inform you when something suitable comes on the market. Many estate agents have a number of developers on their books that are always on the look-out for building sites, so the value of having a good relationship with the estate agent should not be underestimated.

Websites

One of the easiest ways to search for property is to use the internet. Many estate agents now have websites and there are websites that cover groups of estate agents. Some websites advertise property for sale right across the British Isles and beyond. The best websites allow you to search by area, property type, value or estate agent. When you have identified a site that you think may be of interest, contact the estate agent or vendor as appropriate and make arrange-ments to visit it.

Auctions

Some sites are sold by public auction. Keep an eye on the local papers or in local estate agents for details of auctions; sometimes they are held on the property, sometimes in a hotel or public hall. Some auction houses publish guide prices on property, but such prices do not mean that the site will sell for that price. Guide prices are often deliberately set low to attract interest and to encourage a bidding frenzy. Do not get carried away with bidding. Decide on what the value of the piece of land is before the auction and be prepared to walk away if the bidding goes above that figure. Do your homework on the site before you are even tempted to bid at an auction. At the fall of the hammer, a legal contract comes into existence between the purchaser and the vendor, whereby the purchaser is deemed to have accepted all of the terms and conditions of the sale. It is normal practice to have to pay a ten per cent deposit on the purchase price so you should have funds to hand when you are serious about bidding at an auction. If you then change your mind and prevaricate on com-pleting the sale by the agreed date, you will be charged interest at around five per cent above the base lending rate and if you pull out completely, you are liable to be sued for the full costs of re-advertising and the sale of the property, including any potential

Site with ruin that may be suitable for a replacement dwelling.

shortfall in its value due to the resale. Most sites for sale by auction will have a reserve price but this may not be advertised. If the bids do not reach the reserve price on the day of the auction, the auctioneer may withdraw the property from sale. Be prepared to raise your bid up to your maximum, even if you are the only one bidding, in order to get over the reserve if required.

Some auctions are held by telephone but do not hold the same legal status as one held in an auction room as the contract is not binding until it is physically exchanged. This can lead to erroneous bids and gazumping where you may be outbid by a prospective purchaser who does not complete the exchange of contracts required.

Planning Registry

If you are looking for a site that has the benefit of planning permission then the local planning office is a good place to start. Visit the planning office and ask to have a look at the planning register for the area. The nature of planning is that any application is deemed to be in the public domain and therefore can be viewed as an 'open file'. This will identify all planning applications that have been successful and give you details of who made the applications and on whose behalf. In most cases, sites on the register will be developed by the person named on the planning application, but not always. It may just be that the owner is simply trying to increase the value of the land prior to placing it on the market. Noting down the contact details, and giving the owners a call to enquire as to the availability of the sites, can be a worthwhile exercise. It may even be possible to obtain a site before it is placed on the open market. While inspecting the register, you will be able to see

Site in rear garden of self-builder's house.

the type of developments that are receiving planning permission in the area in which you are looking. Outline applications will have a location plan, description of access requirements and a description of the proposed development. Full applications will have plans, sections and elevations of the proposed house, as well as a written component describing the materials to be used. If you live in a house with a very large garden you may be living right on top of your new site. Providing the site area is large enough to sub-divide and you can obtain access and planning permission, then you may be able to live in your own house and supervise the work while building your new sustainable home.

LAND VALUE

Before you part with your hard earned cash you will want to make sure that the piece of land you are buying is value for money. The rule of thumb for land valuation for building sites is based on an estimated market value of a house on the site, minus the cost of building such a house. Obviously there are a number of unknown factors associated with this type of valuation such as the size of house that can be built on the site, but because you know the size of house you want to build, it should be fairly straightforward for you to work out whether the land represents value for money for your needs. It goes without saying that if the market value of your finished house far outweighs the site purchase price plus the cost of building then the decision should be easy to make.

OWNERSHIP

Once you have identified the piece of ground you want to build on, and if you do not already own it, you have to either lease the ground or purchase it. To purchase a piece of land you will require the title of the ground to be transferred to your ownership. The instrument used to transfer title from one person to another is called a property deed and conveyancing is the term used for the act of transfer of legal title. The work surrounding the transfer of title is normally carried out by a solicitor as the structure and wording of the documentation is written in legal terms and requires meticulous attention to detail. It is possible,

however, for a person who knows what they are doing to do their own conveyancing.

Appointing a Solicitor

When it comes to the point that you place an offer on a site (or immediately prior to that in Scotland) you should appoint a solicitor to do the conveyancing for you. As with every professional appointment, you should appoint a solicitor who has experience in doing the type of work that you wish to commission them to do. A solicitor who specializes in conveyancing should be more efficient and therefore more cost effective than one who specializes in some other aspect of the law but, as with every commission, you should shop around to get the best deal. Your solicitor will conduct searches to identify the ownership of the plot and any covenants, rights of way or other issues that may affect the piece of land. Your solicitor should also be able to advise you how to make an initial offer in writing to the vendor, subject to contract if appropriate. The offer may include a timescale to allow additional information to be gathered on the site such as planning, site conditions and others.

Title

It is important that the piece of land you are interested in can actually be sold. If there is some form of dispute over the title, such as often occurs when there is more than one interest registered against a piece of land, then it may be a number of years before ownership of the title can be established, so buyer beware. Remember too that not all land that is being sold is 'freehold' and if the land is 'leasehold', then it will revert back to the freeholder on expiry of the lease. Just make sure in such circumstances that there is sufficient time left on the lease to allow you to get full use or to sell the property on without its value being affected by a very short lease. If the length of lease is an issue you can often negotiate a longer lease with the vendor, but again this can take some time to complete. Once again, your solicitor should be able to provide you with all the relevant information regarding the title.

Charges

The ideal piece of land has no charges or covenants

55

and is said to be 'unencumbered'. Because land can be used as surety for a loan or other business transaction, the person who has given the loan has taken out a charge against the land so that when it is sold, they have the first call against any monies raised in the sale. In most cases the settlement of such charges upon sale is straightforward, but if there are old charges that have not been settled then it can raise some difficulties; in these cases you should take advice from your solicitor as there are solutions to such issues.

There are a number of conditions that can be attached to the title such as covenants, way leaves and easements. These are put in place when a third party has some right over the piece of land.

Covenants

Check for covenants that may restrict the type, size, location or use of a building. In Scotland these are called burdens.

If the owner cannot be traced or the covenant is now defunct, it may be unlikely that you will be pursued for breaking the terms of the covenant. It may also be possible to take out insurance against someone pursuing you for damages for breaking the terms of the covenant.

Rights of Way, Way-leaves and Easements

Boundary Disputes

It is not uncommon for the legal boundaries to a piece of land to be slightly different from the physical boundaries currently on site. Over the years, as fences and walls have been erected and re-erected, the positions may have changed slightly. The title deeds should have a record of the boundaries that relate to the land, and it is worth checking the actual boundaries against those shown on the title. If there are any discrepancies between the title and the piece of land being offered, then these should be cleared up before completing the purchase. Sometimes the discrepancies are important, for example gaining sight lines for access to the site, but in other circumstances the discrepancies are entirely inconsequential.

Party Walls

The Party Wall Act of 1996 applies to England and Wales and provides a framework for the prevention and resolution of disputes in relation to party walls and associated boundary conditions. In simple terms it states that when one party is doing work that affects a party wall, then notice must be given in writing to the other party. A notice period of two months applies and if an adjoining owner responds to your notice or issues a counter notice within fourteen days, a dispute is deemed to have arisen. The Act gives a list of works that can be carried out to a party wall that go beyond common law rights. It also clearly defines what work cannot be carried out. The Act allows for foundations of a new party wall to intrude under neighbouring land, but subject to payment for any damage that may have been caused during the work. The Act also covers excavations close to neighbouring buildings such that you must again give two months written notice before you (within three metres of a neighbouring building or structure) excavate or construct your foundations deeper than your neighbours; or within six metres of a neighbouring building or structure excavate or construct your foundations deeper than a line drawn at 45° downwards from the bottom of the neighbouring foundations. The purpose of this aspect of the Act is to ensure that your excavations do not unintentionally undermine or destabilize your neighbours' foundations.

Site Access

One of the first things that you should check is that there is not 'ransom strip' between your proposed site and the public highway. A ransom strip is a small, often narrow, strip of land area adjacent to your plot that must be crossed to enable you to access the land. A further consideration is the provision of sight lines for an access. If you do not have control over the land adjacent to the proposed access point, you may not be able to satisfy the Roads Service Development Control Section as to the compliance of the access. You may need to pay a ransom to achieve the required sight lines.

Planning Permission

Be careful that the piece of land that you are purchasing either has or is likely to get planning permission. There are unscrupulous vendors who will advertise land with promises that sound as if planning permission is just a matter of applying and it will be granted. You can of course add the condition to the sale that completion will be subject to suitable planning permission being granted. Furthermore, if the plot has the benefit of planning permission, check carefully the conditions that are attached to the consent to ensure that you will be able to build the type of house that you want on the site in the position that you want it. A site sold with full planning permission will have a full design associated with the consent granted, whereas a site sold with just outline planning permission will have permission to develop the land in principle only, and generally with conditions attached.

Tree Preservation Orders (TPOs) and Wildlife Orders

Tree Preservation Orders are placed on trees that are considered to be an integral part of the character of an area or that contribute to the setting of a listed building.

Be sure that the TPOs do not pose such a restriction on the site that it becomes impossible to develop. This applies to site access as well as to the proposed house footprint. Remember too that the roots of a tree which has a TPO should not be disturbed, and as a rule of thumb, the root spread is roughly equivalent to the spread of the crown. If you must remove a tree that does not have a TPO then you should plant two in its place. Wildlife orders have the same effect as TPOs and are set in place to ensure that endangered species are adequately protected.

PURCHASING A PLOT IN ENGLAND AND WALES

In the United Kingdom, all land was once held by the Crown, and was then parcelled out at various times to a variety of subjects and then sold on piecemeal. Today land is generally sold on the basis of 'private treaty'. Details of the piece of land to be sold are gathered together and the land is offered for sale as an 'invitation to treat'. In England and Wales an offer can be made on a plot that is already under offer.

When it comes to making an offer for a piece of land, your offer should be made 'subject to contract' and if the offer is acceptable to the vendor then the offer is accepted subject to contract. When making a purchase you should instruct your solicitor to draft up a contract and a list of preliminary enquiries. Your solicitor will exchange letters and enquiries with the vendor's solicitors, obtain the required searches and report the findings to you. If you have not done so already, you should arrange for a survey. If you need

Check if the trees are protected by Tree Preservation Orders (TPOs).

to raise finances, you should approach your mortgage or other lending company and organize funds. If the price is right and the conditions of the contract are acceptable then the parties exchange contracts. This is done by each party signing identical copies of the contract, which are then exchanged. Generally a ten per cent deposit exchanges hands at the point of exchange of contracts and a completion date is set. The vendor signs the conveyance and the final monies are paid over on the completion date, at which point you, the purchaser, will take possession of your land. It is a legal requirement that the transaction is registered in the Land Registry Office and the relevant stamp duty paid if required.

PURCHASING A PLOT IN NORTHERN IRELAND

The Northern Irish system of tenure follows that of England and Wales with a few minor variations. Contracts are not exchanged; instead of this, when the parties have agreed a price and the conditions and when all searches and so forth have been made, the purchaser signs the contract which is then countersigned by the vendor. When the contract is returned to the purchaser, a contract is deemed to be in place between the parties.

PURCHASING A PLOT IN SCOTLAND

In Scotland, the land holding system is slightly different from the rest of the UK and the terminology used in relation to conveyancing is somewhat different too. Most land transactions are conducted by formal tender, as follows. Properties are generally advertised for sale through solicitors in much the same way as estate agents advertise land for sale by private treaty south of the border. As a purchaser you decide what price you are prepared to offer, which can be below or above the advertised price, and you instruct your solicitor to make a formal offer and register an interest in the property. In Scotland, once a property is under offer, no further offers can be accepted unless the sale falls through. There is then an obligation on the vendor to inform you if there is a better offer from another prospective purchaser, or

to tell you if the property has been sold. If the price offered is acceptable to the vendor, you should then get a survey and valuation undertaken and when you have the necessary monies in place your solicitor will then proceed to make a written offer which will include the completion date and any other conditions to which the purchase will be subject. These 'Missives', as they are known, are much the same as conditions and preliminary enquiries in England and Wales. If the written offer is accepted by the vendor, then the offer is binding on both parties, unless there are discrepancies or disagreements in the missives negotiations. When everything is agreed by both parties, the 'Disposition' is signed and 'Date of Entry' or completion date is agreed. On the completion date the monies due are handed over and the purchaser takes possession. The solicitor will take care of registering the transaction and payment of stamp duty where required.

PURCHASING A PLOT IN SOUTHERN IRELAND

Once again the system of buying land in the Republic of Ireland is very similar to the United Kingdom of Great Britain and Northern Ireland. There are some minor variations in the wording and normally a booking or holding fee of five per cent of the purchase price is paid on verbal agreement with an additional five per cent paid on signing the contract. In addition, the title is not investigated until after the contract is signed, similar to the Scottish system. If something is uncovered which affects the title in an unsatisfactory manner, then the contract is voided, otherwise the completion of the sale is much the same as in the rest of the British Isles.

Insuring the Site

Make sure that as soon as you have completed the transaction of purchasing your plot of land that you take out insurance. Remember that you will be held responsible for the safety of anyone on your land and remember too that building sites are dangerous places, so with this in mind it is worth erecting fencing around the site to secure it and putting up health and safety signs at the same time to warn others of the dangers of entering a building site.

CONCLUSION

This chapter has identified a number of locations and methods for finding your ideal site. Sites can appear on any of them at any time so it is worth keeping an eye on a number of them. Having identified a site that you are interested in, you should make an offer if appropriate or appoint a solicitor to place the offer on your behalf. Your solicitor will carry out the relevant checks regarding ownership and the extent of the title. Things to look out for when purchasing a site include potential issues with party walls and site access, tree preservation orders and wildlife orders. You should also satisfy yourself regarding the likelihood of obtaining planning permission if it has not already been obtained. Having made your purchase, you should insure the site and begin the design process in earnest. Chapter Six will look at the design process in detail.

sustainable home, but for the purposes of this book we will concentrate on those issues that are considered important enough to be included in many of the environmental assessment methods available today and in particular The Code for Sustainable Homes introduced in Chapter 1. Remembering that The Code for Sustainable Homes is intended by the United Kingdom Government to become mandatory, if you give due consideration to each of these issues now, you will be able to measure in a recognized way, just how sustainable your house really is.

SUSTAINABILITY ISSUES

Energy and CO_2 Emissions

At the top of the agenda are Energy and CO_2 emissions. The reason for this being so important is that after all of the other issues have been addressed, your house will continue to consume energy and produce CO_2 emissions for the rest of its life. Thus, next to a holistic approach, it is the single most important aspect of sustainable design.

A sustainably designed house will use a minimum amount of energy throughout its life, and will produce a minimum amount of CO_2. To do this it will have to rely more heavily on renewable energy than conventional energy.

Most conventional energy sources rely on the burning of fossil fuels and this has two main effects.

Firstly, it depletes a finite resource and at some point the supply will run out or become too expensive and difficult to extract. Secondly, the burning of fossil fuels produces pollution and greenhouse gases which contribute to global warming.

Because this issue is so important it will not be covered in detail here but instead has been allocated a full chapter on its own. Chapter 7 deals with designing for energy efficiency in detail. Remember though, that it must be considered as only one part of a sustainable design strategy, and if considered on its own, you may well design an energy efficient house but more than likely it will not be as sustainable as it could have been.

Dwelling Emission Rate (mandatory)
The Dwelling Emission Rate (DER) is now a requirement of building control and is an estimate of how much CO_2 per square metre of floor area will be emitted to the atmosphere arising from a notional operation of the house and associated services (primarily space and water heating). In designing a sustainable house you should be trying to limit the emissions of carbon dioxide (CO_2) into the atmosphere that arise from what is assumed to be the normal operation of a dwelling and its services. To do this, the building fabric will be required to be well insulated to cut down on fabric heat loss; the building will be required to be airtight to reduce

A small roof-mounted wind turbine at the BRE Innovation Park.

Heat recovery unit of a whole house ventilation system.

Code Level 6 rated Kingspan Lighthouse at the BRE Innovation Park.

Insulated door on the Kingspan Lighthouse.

infiltration heat loss and will require efficient lighting and heating appliances, preferably low carbon or zero carbon. The use of a whole house ventilation system with heat recovery will result in a slightly lower DER.

This is because the calculations rightly account for the extra electricity that is used to power the fans in such a system, but remember that the benefits of whole house heat recovery far outweigh the drawbacks; always keep in the back of your mind that sustainable design involves a holistic approach to the many and often competing issues. The dwelling emission rate is linked directly to the amount and type of energy and also the performance of the building fabric. To achieve The Code for Sustainable Homes Code 6, zero carbon status must be achieved. This means that, in addition to negating CO_2 from lighting, space heating and water heating, CO_2 emissions from all cooking and other domestic appliances must also be accounted for.

Building fabric
A sustainably designed house will future-proof the home's energy efficiency over its whole life by limiting heat losses across the building envelope. This is achieved by increasing insulation levels well beyond that required by Building Control (remember that building control standards are statutory minimum standards only). Chapter Seven shows how this can be achieved and overviews a range of insulation materials that can be used. To achieve The Code for Sustainable Homes Code 6, opaque elements in roofs, walls and exposed floors should achieve a maximum U-Value of $0.13W/m^2.K$, while windows should achieve a BFRC (British Fenestration Rating Council) rating in the A band or better. Doors should achieve U-values better than $1.513W/m^2.K$ if glazed or $1.013W/m^2.K$ if solid.

Internal Lighting
Daylight is a free resource that should be utilized to

the fullest extent, but artificial lighting will obviously be required during periods when daylight is not available. Your objective here is to provide energy efficient internal lighting with a view to reducing the amount of CO_2 emissions that the dwelling is responsible for. Before the advent of compact fluorescent light fittings, the heat produced by traditional tungsten lamps was considered as an incidental heat gain that contributed to the heating of the house. The problem with this approach is that the heat from a tungsten lamp is being generated using electricity where the primary production of electricity at the power station and subsequent transmission to your house results in greater CO_2 emissions compared with generating the same amount of heat with an energy-efficient and low carbon-heating source within the dwelling itself. To achieve The Code for Sustainable Homes Code 6, 100 per cent of the light fittings should be low energy fittings.

Retractable washing line for an outdoor drying space.

Drying Space

In the process of drying clothes tumble dryers use a great deal of energy and in doing so produce a great deal of CO_2. It is good practice therefore to provide a reduced energy means of drying clothes such as an outside clothes line. If your house design incorpo-

rates mechanical ventilation with heat recovery it is also possible to have a drying area within the dwelling that utilizes the resulting air movement. Freshly warmed air can be delivered to the drying area, and the damp warm air removed and the heat recovered. Remember that a holistic view of the design will find more than one use for the individual elements.

Energy labelled white goods

Bearing in mind that the majority of our electricity is produced by the burning of fossil fuels, this requirement is to encourage the provision or purchase of energy efficient white goods, and therefore reduce the CO_2 emissions from appliances in the dwelling. Ensure that all of your white goods are 'energy saving recommended' and are in the 'A' band as these are the most energy efficient.

External lighting

There is little point in providing energy efficient lighting inside the house if the total energy consumed by these pales into insignificance compared to a single external high power light fitting as seen on many properties. This requirement is to encourage the provision of energy efficient external lighting, and once again reduce associated CO_2 emissions. The advent of powerful compact fluorescent external lights means that the same lighting levels can be achieved using a fraction of the energy.

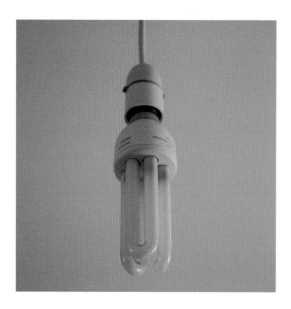

Low-energy light fitting.

Low-energy bulb in external light fitting.

Solar water heating panels on the roof of the Osborne Demonstration House at BRE.

Low or Zero Carbon (LZC) Technologies

By encouraging local energy generation from renewable sources to supply a significant proportion of the energy demand, there will be a corresponding reduction in carbon emissions and atmospheric pollution. Technologies such as solar water heating, solar photovoltaics, wind power and use of air and ground source heat pumps are deemed to be low carbon technologies. To achieve The Code for Sustainable Homes Code 6 along with all of the other requirements of the code you will need to produce as much energy on your site as you consume; that is your house will need to be carbon neutral. To do this you will need to use solar water heaters for your domestic hot water, and also produce electricity using solar photovoltaic panels.

Cycle Storage

The majority of all car journeys made are less than five miles. When bicycles are used for transport then there is a corresponding reduction in the use of fossil fuels. The provision of adequate and secure cycle storage facilities is thus deemed to reduce the need for short car journeys and to encourage the wider use of bicycles. Of course this will only result in a reduction of carbon dioxide if you actually use your bicycle for such journeys.

Covered cycle storage area in rear garden.

Home Office

The ability to work from home can reduce the need to commute to work. To assist with working from home, provision of a home office should be made and the associated services to allow for working from

65

home. Even if your own working circumstances preclude working from home, you should consider future-proofing the house to allow for others to work from home at some point.

Pollution

Global Warming Potential (GWP) of Insulants

Insulation comes in many forms and materials, some of which are more environmentally friendly than others. Foamed thermal and acoustic insulating materials that use blowing agents that contribute to atmospheric pollution or global warming should be avoided. Only purchase insulation materials that have minimal or no GWP.

NOx Emissions

The emission of nitrogen oxides (NOx) into the atmosphere is a major source of air pollution. These gases are the result of burning fossil fuels at high temperatures such as in car engines and in domestic boilers. Some of the modern condensing boilers on the market today produce minimal quantities of NOx; some as low as five parts per million (PPM), and if you are intent on having a boiler, then this is the type of boiler that you should use.

Water

Water is a precious resource, even in the UK and Ireland. The commonly held view is that there is no shortage of rainfall in these islands and water is therefore not an issue, even though there have been water shortages in the past. Water collected in our reservoirs from rain appears to be in plenteous supply, and because traditionally payments for water have been subsumed in local authority taxes, it is commonly assumed that water is free. This is not the case. Clean potable water as supplied by the public utility companies is very expensive to produce. Filtering and pumping consume vast quantities of energy; energy that for the most part is produced from the burning of fossil fuels. The advent of domestic water meters is making individual households accountable for their water use.

Internal Water Use (Mandatory)

Anything that can be done to reduce the consump-

tion of potable water in the home is of benefit. To achieve The Code for Sustainable Homes Code 6, the maximum water consumption allowed is 80 litres per person per day. The amount of water used within the dwelling can be reduced by using fittings that reduce water use in WCs, taps and showers. Further reductions can be achieved by installing grey water or rain water collection and treatment systems for use where the use of potable water would be a waste.

External Water Use

A system to collect rainwater for use in irrigation should be provided to encourage the recycling of rainwater and reduce the amount of mains potable water used for external water purposes. This can be as simple as collecting rain in a rain water butt, or as complex as a central rainwater collection tank and plumbing to the intended use points.

Rainwater collection from roof run-off.

Surface Water Run-off

Management of Surface Water Run-off from Developments (mandatory)

This can be achieved by designing your house and garden and hard landscaping areas to avoid, reduce and delay the discharge of rainfall to public sewers and watercourses. This has the effect of not only protecting watercourses and reducing the risk of localized flooding, but also reduces pollution and other environmental damage.

Green roofs help to attenuate surface water run-off.

Roof lights help achieve high levels of daylighting.

Flood Risk

Where possible you should select a site that is in a low flood-risk area. If, however, your house is in a medium or high risk area you should provide appropriate measures to reduce the impact of flooding on houses built in areas with a medium or high flood risk, including ensuring safe access and escape routes and flood resilient and resistant construction.

Heath and Wellbeing

Daylighting

It is a well documented fact that the human eye responds better to daylight than to artificial light and it is equally well known that there are health and physiological benefits associated with daylight. By providing good daylighting the need for energy to light the home will also be reduced. At the very minimum all living rooms, dining rooms, studies, and home offices should be provided with adequate daylight. It is also possible to get daylight deep into the plan of a house by using roof lights or other high level glazing.

Sound Insulation

One of the most common causes for disputes between neighbours is the problem of noise. To ensure that you are not a nuisance neighbour, you should provide improved sound insulation above that

The build up of your walls will determine the level of sound insulation.

required in the building regulations. This will reduce the likelihood of noise complaints from your neighbours.

Private Space

The purpose of this requirement is to improve the occupiers' quality of life by providing an outdoor space for their use, which is at least partially private. This may be in the form of a terrace, patio, garden, backyard or play area for children.

67

Private amenity space at the rear of a property.

Cedar cladding and hemp lime render add to the sustainability credentials of this house.

Lifetime Homes (Mandatory for Code 4 and Above)

The Lifetime Homes concept was developed by the Habinteg Housing Association and includes sixteen criteria that enable homes to be accessible to a wide range of occupants including elderly and many disabled people, and that can be easily adapted when required to meet the changing needs of a household. The concept recognizes that as people get older they become less able to access their house as they did when they were younger and if adaptations can be made that will allow continued occupation then it will encourage people to stay in their own community.

Materials

Some materials are considered more sustainable than others. The materials that are used for both major building elements and finishing elements can have a significant influence on the overall environmental impact of your house.

Environmental Impact of Materials (Mandatory)

The Building Research Establishment has developed a Green Guide to Specification (access to which is available free online), which considers the life cycle assessment (LCA) or cradle-to-grave environmental impact of materials. Materials are rated from A+ at their best to D at their worst. When choosing the materials for your house, choose only those materials that have a good environmental rating as these will have lower environmental impacts over their lifecycle.

Responsible Sourcing of Materials – Building Elements

The specification of key building elements should be based on materials that are responsibly sourced, including the ground floor, upper floors (including separating floors), roof, external walls, internal walls (including separating walls), foundation/substructure (excluding sub-base materials) and the staircase.

Quality natural slate has a long life expectancy.

Additionally, 100 per cent of any timber in any of the above elements must be legally sourced. Further information on the responsible sourcing of materials can be found on the BRE website.

Responsibly sourced cedar cladding.

Responsible Sourcing of Materials – Finishing Elements

The specification of finishing elements, such as stairs, windows, external and internal doors, skirting, panelling, furniture, fascias and any other significant use should insist on timber from certified sustainable sources.

Additionally, 100 per cent of any timber used in these elements must be legally sourced.

Insulation materials are covered in greater depth in Chapter Seven.

Alternative Construction Methods and Materials

There are a number of tried and trusted ways of using environmentally-benign building materials in non-conventional ways that you may wish to consider if you are prepared to do most of, if not all of, the building work, or at the very least the supervision of the building work yourself. The reason being that if you were to ask a traditional builder to carry out such work they would not even know where to begin. Since there are many books written in great detail about each of the following non- conventional ways of building, we will provide here only a brief overview for your consideration.

Rammed earth walls have a particularly homely feel.

Construction Site Impacts

The very act of building on a site can have a significant environmental impact in terms of energy use, water use, disturbance and dust pollution to air and waste. You should ensure that your site is managed in a manner that mitigates these environmental impacts.

Security

In designing your home, it is important to take into consideration the overall impact of your house on the security and safety of the neighbourhood in which you are building. Each police force throughout the country will have a crime prevention design advisor who can provide free advice on how to design your home to comply with the requirements of 'Secured by Design – new Homes'. The purpose of this is to encourage design where people feel safe and secure; where crime and disorder, or the fear of crime, does not undermine the overall quality of life or community cohesion.

Ecology

Ecological Value of Site

If you can build on land that has limited value to wildlife then when you build you will have minimal impact. The ecological value of a site is obviously affected by its previous use. A site that has been built on previously or perhaps an area of hard standing is better to build on from an ecological perspective than a green field site. The presence of ecological features such as trees, hedges, watercourses, wetlands, meadows and so on should not be taken for granted either, and these features should be protected where at all possible. By doing this you will help to slow down the destruction of the existing natural habitats and the wildlife they support, as well as helping to prevent the loss of land that can be used for agriculture and parkland.

Ecological Enhancement

Careful consideration should be given to enhancing the ecological value of your site by introducing appropriate plant species and habitats. This is an area of specialist expertise and a suitably qualified ecologist should be consulted if you do not have the required expertise yourself. Remember that attracting wildlife to your garden will be difficult or nigh impossible if the garden consists mainly of a driveway and closely cropped lawns.

Protection of Ecological Features

Any existing ecological features on the site should be protected from substantial damage during the clearing of the site and the completion of construction works. This may include protecting 'wild' areas, maintaining native species, and protecting trees from accidental damage during the construction process.

Change in Ecological Value of Site

Steps should be taken to minimize the reduction in the ecological value of a site and to encourage an improvement in the ecological value by introducing greater biodiversity. Aim to improve the overall ecological value so that your house makes a positive contribution to the environment.

Building Footprint

One way to reduce the footprint of a house is to build more than one storey. This has the obvious effect of not only reducing the ground floor area and thus the area of the site that is used up, but also reducing the roof area as well. Generally a two-storey house will have less material in the foundations, but slightly more in the external walls. There will also be the need for a stair, which takes up valuable floor space, but having said all this, it is generally more economical to build a two-storey house than to build a single-storey house of the same floor area. One further consideration is that compared to a single-storey house, a two-storey house has less overall surface area exposed to the elements, and is therefore more energy efficient.

There is considerable value in creating a basement in new houses, particularly where high land values and small building plots restrict the building footprint. Basements have many benefits including providing additional space for growing families which may allow your family to stay in one location without having to move. Furthermore, basements are useful areas for locating such technologies as thermal stores, rainwater harvesting tanks and even compost toilet holding tanks. The main drawback with a basement, however, is that it can be difficult to exclude

Storey and a half house reduces both building footprint and surface area.

groundwater, particularly where the water-table is high, and great attention to detail is required to ensure continuity and longevity of the tanking membrane. Excavated soil from a basement should be spread on the site where possible or used to create a landscape feature to prevent unnecessary transport and additions to landfill.

One other way in which to reduce the footprint of your house is to provide rooms in the roof. This is one of the cheapest ways of creating floor space, since you will be building a roof anyway as part of the external envelope of the house.

Waste
Storage of Non-recyclable Waste and
Recyclable Household Waste (mandatory)
Adequate storage space should be provided both indoors and outdoors for the storage of non-recyclable waste and recyclable household waste.

The Stewart Milne Group's four-storey Sigma House designed to reduce building footprint.

Construction waste Management
(Mandatory)

Waste should be carefully controlled on site to reduce the quantity that goes to landfill. To do this it is important that you develop and implement a waste management plan. The plan should set targets for promoting efficiency. Waste should be segregated into waste types and any that can be recycled should be forwarded to the relevant agency.

Composting

If you have the space you should provide facilities to compost household waste, thus reducing the amount of household waste sent to landfill. The added bonus of composting household waste is that you will have a ready supply of good organic compost to add to your garden. If you are not a keen gardener, there are plenty of keen gardeners around who would be only too happy to take good compost off your hands.

CONCLUSION

This chapter has acknowledged that every time we build a house, we use up ground; we disturb existing ecosystems; we create pollution and use energy in the building process; we use up water; we use up the earth's resources in the supply of building materials; and we produce waste. The chapter has also shown that it is possible however to have minimal impact on the environment so that when you are building your own home you can incorporate each of mitigating measures to minimize the overall environmental impact of your home.

CHAPTER SEVEN

Design for Energy Efficiency

Since energy efficiency and CO$_2$ emissions are such an important issue in designing a sustainable home, this chapter examines the design requirements for energy efficiency under three main headings: site layout, the building envelope and building services. It emphasises in particular: the relative importance of insulation; free energy and energy storage for both timber frame and masonry construcion; and identifies how energy efficiency can be achieved for different types of masonry and timber frame construction, regardless of site layout. It then looks at energy-efficient building methods that provide passive solar heating and/or cooling, and discusses building services systems such as mechanical ventilation with heat recovery, solar hot water heating, photovoltaics, and grey water recycling.

We live in a climate where some form of heating is on average required for some eight months out of twelve. To date, the majority of this heating has come from the burning of fossil fuels with resulting emissions to the atmosphere of harmful gases such as CO$_2$ and NO$_x$, which are known to have an effect on climate change. Couple this with the fact that fossil fuels are predicted to run out in the near future and that prices for them keep on rising, then it makes sense to minimize our reliance on them. To do this there are a number of basic principles to follow in designing the overall site layout, creating the building envelope and also designing the building services for your house. These are respectively: create a site layout that allows access to the sun and provides shelter from the wind; use less energy by creating a highly efficient building envelope; make use of free heat gains from the sun, appliances and activities that take place within the house; store any excess heat within the building fabric; recover heat from ventilation air that might otherwise be lost; use solar water heating where possible and consider the use of other renewable technologies such as

ground source heat pumps, wind turbines and others.

If you are designing your own house, then you should endeavour to follow the above principles. To make your job a little easier they have been placed in order of consideration and importance. Should you find however, as is often the case, that there is a conflict between some of the issues, you should consider the order of importance before making a value judgement as to where a compromise can be reached. Remember that if you get the big decisions right, the smaller decisions don't matter so much; but if you get the big decisions wrong then no amount of fiddling with the smaller decisions will make up for the more important aspects.

If you are employing an architect to design your house for you (highly recommended), then use this chapter as a briefing document to let the architect know what it is that you want from your house, and use it as an aide-memoire to criticise the architect's proposals. Before you do employ an architect however, as with anyone else you employ, check out what energy efficient buildings they have worked on in the past and only make your choice when you are satisfied that they can achieve what you want from your house. Architects have been trained to create aesthetically pleasing design solutions to meet specific requirements and, if you are not specific enough, then you will get what the architect wants or what the architect thinks you want, rather than what you really want. Architects have also been trained to deal with criticism, so if the design does not meet the brief or if the design is not to your liking, then let the architect know and in the first instance have them explain why the design is the way it is. If the explanation accords with reason then so be it, but if not then have them revise the design to suit your requirements.

Remember that space heating and water heating combined make up the greatest proportion of house-

hold energy consumption, so we will concentrate on heating in this chapter. Before tackling the issues however, it is useful to remind ourselves of how heat is lost from a house.

If the temperature outdoors is lower than the temperature indoors, as is the case for most of the year in the UK and Ireland, then heat from inside will flow outwards and this heat is considered as being lost. Normally the greatest amount of heat is lost through the building envelope, the roof, walls, windows, doors and floors, and this is normally referred to as 'building fabric heat loss'. Heat is also lost through ventilation as the air being replaced in the house carries heat with

The Kingspan Lighthouse at BRE utilizes multiple renewable energy technologies.

South-facing amenity areas will catch the sun.

it and the air replacing it has to be heated to room temperature. This is known as ventilation heat loss. Heat lost through air that manages to find its way through the building fabric during windy conditions is called infiltration heat loss.

SITE LAYOUT

Access to Solar Radiation and Daylight

The primary objectives with site layout are two-fold: to provide a layout that promotes passive solar design and enhances the energy and the environmental performance of the house; and at the same time to increase the amenity value of the site.

Site Zoning

The first thing to do after completing the site analysis

is to zone the site. Some sites are so small or otherwise restricted that most decisions relating to zoning of the site have already been made for you – for example the site can only be accessed from one particular point, and a house can only just be squeezed into what is left of the site in one particular area with one particulate orientation. If this is the case then you can concentrate your design decisions on the layout of the house itself. If, on the other hand, your site gives you some freedom to choose the location and orientation of your house then site layout is the first decision that you should make.

Increasing the Amenity Value of Your Site

Most people like to have direct access to an area outside the house where they can sit and relax and enjoy outdoor activities as and when the weather permits. This should ideally be located on the sunny

77

side of the house and should complement the house layout to create a pleasant indoor/outdoor flow.

To achieve this, the house should be located towards the north part of the site allowing the amenity space to be towards the south. There may however be a conflict between creating a south-facing private amenity space and privacy, particularly if the south side of the house faces a road. If the site is large enough then a well laid out garden with fences, walls and screen planting will create enough privacy, but be careful not to cause over-shading of the amenity space. Site constraints however, may mean that the only area available for outdoor use is to the east, west or north. In this case the outdoor area should where possible be located just beyond where shading from the house will occur during the hours when the outdoor space will most likely be used.

Building Orientation

The area shaded from the sun to the north of passive solar houses can be used for vehicular access, car parking and ancillary buildings to provide a buffer zone. The east, west and the south elevations are of course the best elevations for receiving year round solar energy in the form of direct sunlight. To promote the utilization of this solar energy one must first allow sunlight to reach the windows. If the windows are orientated within 30° of due south then they will be able to collect what little solar energy there is available in winter. One of the challenges associated with site layout, however, is that there can be a conflict between providing shelter from the wind and at the same time providing solar access. Shelterbelts and windbreaks around your house will have the effect of reducing wind speed all the way around the house and will also cut down on building fabric heat loss and infiltration heat loss. In most cases the conflict between wind shelter and solar access can be resolved by increasing the distance between the building and the wind shelter. This is particularly important if the wind shelter is within 30° of due south. As well as providing wind shelters in windy locations you could also consider providing shrubs and vegetation around the house to increase surface roughness thereby improving site wind climate without prejudicing solar gain. In a few situations, such as highly exposed sites on the crests of hills and on north facing slopes, the demands of solar access and microclimate cannot both be met. Here it may be best to concentrate on improving site microclimate and providing enough daylight and sunlight for amenity purposes. One other method that may work in such an exposed location is to build an enclosed courtyard with the house opening out on to it to the south. The surfaces chosen within the courtyard can then reflect or absorb solar gain as required.

Choice of External Materials

Materials used on the ground immediately around your house can help with allowing solar energy to be utilized within the house. If the materials are light in colour and reflect light, this will increase the amount of light incident on the windows thereby increasing the amount of solar gain. One other advantage is that because the light is being reflected in an upwards direction, the light entering the window tends to be reflected onto the ceiling making it brighter and allowing the light to penetrate further into the room.

THE BUILDING ENVELOPE

Imagine a person who lives outdoors 24/7 and 365 days a year. Imagine further that the person only has one set of clothes to wear for the whole year and that the clothes cannot be changed at any time during the year. Now picture the building envelope as that person's clothing. It has to keep the occupant comfortable all year round, warm and cosy in winter and not too warm in summer. It has to keep out the weather, the wind and the rain and snow. It has to do this without getting a new set of clothes every season. It has to provide some form of ventilation to allow the occupant to breathe, but at the same time be draught free and minimize the amount of heat lost through ventilation. It has to allow light in to allow the occupant to see and at the same time give the occupant a view to the outside. It has to be capable of absorbing moisture generated inside and somehow transporting it to the outside, but at the same time not allowing water from the outside to penetrate to the inside. As you can see, some of the requirements are a little at odds with some of the others. So it is with the envelope of a building.

Compact building form will minimize the surface area and reduce energy demand.

Building Form

From an energy point of view, the most efficient building shape is a very well insulated sphere with no openings whatsoever. This is because for a given volume, a sphere has the least surface area. You will agree however, that building a sphere is not the most practical thing to do, and you would find that even if you could build one, dividing the sphere up into habitable spaces would result in much wasted space, so much so that you would negate any benefits you had gained in the first place. A more buildable form therefore is a cube, but once again we would soon discover that if we tried to fit all the rooms that we wanted into the cube, even a cube is not necessarily the most efficient in terms of space planning so a compromise must be arrived at. What we are trying to achieve is the smallest surface area to volume ratio for a building that is both buildable and that also accommodates all of the spaces required. Thus, most energy efficient buildings end up being rectilinear in shape, are well insulated and usually do not have too many protrusions that would increase the surface area of the building envelope too much. If the long elevation of the house can be orientated towards the south to optimize direct solar gain to rooms, or to other solar technologies, then that is all the better. Items such as dormer windows increase the overall surface area, are difficult to insulate, may make it more difficult to locate solar heating panels and make it more difficult to make the house air tight. The importance of the building envelope cannot be stressed enough because the greater the surface area, the greater the potential for heat loss in winter and heat gain in summer.

However, it is also important to allow for architectural expression and individual style, and as long as we follow a few simple guidelines then there is no reason why your house should not look the way you want it to look, and still be a sustainable and energy-efficient house. It would be a boring world if we all lived in very well insulated boxes that looked exactly the same.

Building Fabric

Timber frame construction and masonry cavity wall construction are the two major construction types for houses in the UK and Ireland. The question is often asked, which is better from an energy efficient point of view? The answer is that it depends on the insulation value of the wall. That simply means that regardless of which type of wall construction you prefer, each can be made to conform to a given insulation level. As with most decisions in constructing your own house, you should weigh up the advantages and disadvantages of each before making a decision. The main difference in timber frame construction and traditional cavity-wall construction is the way in which the inside of the house responds to changes in temperature. A timber-frame house (thermally lightweight) will respond much more quickly to a heat source and will heat up much more quickly than a masonry built house. However, a masonry built house (thermally heavyweight) will cool down much more slowly than a timber frame house because of the heat that has been absorbed by the thermal mass of the internal block-work walls. Your lifestyle will dictate whether your house should be thermally lightweight or thermally heavyweight. If the house is to be occupied on a continuous basis then a thermally heavyweight house will be likely to be the most energy efficient. On the other hand, if the house is to be occupied on an intermittent basis, then a thermally lightweight house will probably be the most energy efficient.

The Four Rules of Passive Solar Design

Regardless of whether your house is to be thermally lightweight or thermally heavyweight, there are four rules to follow when it comes to creating the building envelope of an energy efficient house. These are in order of priority: firstly insulate the building envelope to a high degree to slow down the transfer of heat; secondly, reduce the amount of heat lost through ventilation and air infiltration; thirdly allow free heat gains from the sun to enter the building through openings in the building envelope; and fourthly, provide some form of storage for heat to store free heat gains and reduce temperature swings.

Insulation

In our climate insulation is the single most important aspect of a house that is striving to be energy efficient. Its purpose is to cut down on the rate of heat transfer through the building envelope; to keep the occupants warm in winter and cool in summer. There are some general misconceptions about where insulation should be placed. You have probably heard that you should have the most insulation in the roof because heat rises. Well, heat does rise, but that is only part of the picture. Heat is also transferred horizontally and vertically downwards, so a better approach is to distribute the insulation fairly evenly across the building envelope including the floor, and place slightly more in the roof to allow for the slightly greater heat transfer that takes place there. Picture once again being dressed for the outdoors in winter. You want to be warm in all the right places including your feet. Placing more and more hats on will not make your feet feel much warmer, nor will wearing more pairs of socks make your head much warmer. The overall objective then is to slow down the transfer of heat from inside to outside and vice versa for the whole surface area of the building envelope.

The efficiency with which a material slows down the transfer of heat is inversely proportional to the material's ability to conduct heat. The term used to measure the thermal resistance of a material is the R-value. The better a material conducts heat, the lower the R-value and the poorer it is at insulating, and vice versa. The term used to measure the heat loss through the external envelope is called the 'U-value'. The U-value is simply one over the sum of all the thermal resistances encountered in the heat path. The lower the U-value is, the better the insulating qualities of the wall will be.

In the past, Building Regulations stipulated the minimum average U-value that a building element such as roof, wall or floor had to achieve; however more recently the regulatory authorities have come to appreciate that in trying to improve energy efficiency it is not sufficient to simply achieve a U-value in a particular element, but instead the whole building must be treated as a system of inter-related elements. In the UK this minimum standard for energy efficiency is measured in CO_2 emissions called the Dwelling Emission Rate (Building Emission Rate in Ireland).

Types of Insulation

Insulation for house building is derived from four principle sources: fossil fuels, mineral rock, metals and organic sources. Fossil fuel based insulants include products such as expanded and extruded polystyrene, polyurethane and phenolic foams. Mineral rock based insulants include materials such as vermiculite, perlite, rock wool (fibre) and glass wool (fibre). Metal insulants include multi-foil and vacuum insulation (some foils are metal-coated plastics), and organic insulants include such materials as hemp, sheep's wool, cork, wood fibre, flax and straw.

Insulation materials are produced in three main physical forms, rigid boards, flexible quilts and loose fill. Rigid boards include phenolic foam, expanded polystyrene, and various compressed fibrous materials such as soft board and compressed straw slabs. The most commonly used form of insulation is flexible quilts and includes mineral fibre quilts such as rock wool, glass wool, natural wool and man-made fibre quilts. Loose fill materials include polystyrene beads, cellulose fibres, and chopped and blown rock wool and glass wool. From a sustainability point of view, each of these materials have positive and negative aspects.

Phenolic and Urethane Foams

Some of the best insulating products purely from an efficiency point of view are rigid phenolic and urethane foams, but they are certainly not the most sustainable of materials. They have a very low thermal conductivity, somewhere in the region of 0.018–0.028 W/m°C, which makes them the most thermally efficient insulation product commonly available. In purely practical terms this makes them the thinnest possible insulation board to achieve required U-values. The closed cell structure tends to resist water vapour movement, however phenolic foams can and do become saturated when exposed to moisture, so extra care has to be taken when deciding where to place the insulation layer. The material itself is unaffected by air movement, but if gaps are left between the boards themselves or the boards and the supporting structure, a significant amount of heat can be lost through convective air movement within the spaces, thereby reducing the effectiveness of the insulation by up to half. (This problem can be experienced with other rigid types of insulation as well.) To make matters worse, phenolic foams shrink with time and gaps can become enlarged. The material is

A Structural Insulated Panel (SIP) with extruded polystyrene insulation.

safe and easy to handle but when cutting it with a saw which is the usual method employed, masks will be required as quantities of loose dust are generated. If you do decide that you will use a phenolic foam board then make sure that the board is CFC/HCFC-free with zero Ozone Depletion Potential (ODP).

Rigid Extruded Polystyrene (XPS) Insulation
XPS insulation boasts a thermal conductivity 0.029-

0.036 W/m°C and relatively high compressive strength, making it useful for high-load applications such as beneath concrete floors. It is commonly available in a number of grades to suit a variety of applications. When used beneath a floor slab, XPS provides a smooth stable platform for the DPM. Other positive benefits include being resistant to rot and vermin, being reusable if in reasonable condition, being recyclable through crushing and adding to new sheeting, and the closed cell nature of XPS resists vapour movement. Most blowing agents for XPS manufactured in Europe are zero ozone depletion (ODP). On the negative side, XPS has high embodied energy and is derived from petrochemicals with the resulting resource depletion and pollution risks associated with oil and plastic production. Specifically, styrene and a number of other hydrocarbons are released into the atmosphere during the production process and throughout its life some unstable residues of monomers of styrene may outgas and it may also release small amounts of chlorofluorocarbons. The fire retardant commonly used is HBCD which is classed as being a hazardous material.

Recycled Plastic
You can now buy commercially produced quilt and

External wall with hemp-lime render on soft board sheathing with cellulose infill between studs.

batt insulation that is made primarily from recycled plastic bottles. The plastic insulation material is non-irritant, and is treated to be flame retardant and has a thermal conductivity of approximately 0.040 W/m°C.

If you wish to use the greenest of materials, the choice is limited somewhat and sometimes more expensive initially, but if you want to be as sustainable as possible then you will use the greenest of insulation.

Cellulose Insulation
Cellulose insulation is made primarily from macerated waste paper with small quantities of boric salts added to make it more fire retardant and to help control vermin. It is the least expensive of all the green alternative forms of insulation. It is normally supplied as a loose fill material for loft insulation, but can also be spray applied to the space between timber studs by adding small quantities of water to make the mixture stick. In addition, the loose material can be pumped into cavities, even between studs through holes drilled in the lining materials for this purpose. One drawback in using the material between studs is the tendency for the loose material to settle over time and leave gaps at the top. This can be partially overcome by pumping the cavities under pressure, but this increases the density and reduces the air spaces between the cellulose fibres thus decreasing the insulating qualities somewhat.

Sheep's Wool Insulation
Sheep's wool insulation is made from new and recycled wool and is produced in both batt and rolled blanket formats in a variety of thicknesses. Like cellulose insulation, it is a hygroscopic material and will absorb and desorb water vapour readily and is thus ideal for breathing wall construction. The major advantage of this type of construction is that this process helps keep the house warm in winter and cool in summer. Sheep's wool can be worked with normal tools and is a non-irritant which can be handled without taking any special precautions.

Flax Insulation
The flax plant is grown primarily for extracting linseed oil from the seeds, but in recent years the fibrous stems have been used as insulation in a non-woven matting. As with most fibrous insulation materials, a binding agent is required to ensure the fibrous mat is workable. Starch or textile binders can be used, as can some plastic binding agents. Borates are used as a fire retardant, insecticide and fungicide.

Hemp Insulation
Hemp has good thermal and acoustic properties and has many uses outside the construction industry. It is naturally resistant to insect and fungal attack, but must be treated with Ammonium Phosphate as a fire retardant.

Cork Insulation
Cork is a renewable and recyclable product that is harvested from the bark of cork oak trees on a twenty-five-year cycle and is produced in commercial quantities in Portugal, North Africa and Spain. Because it is derived from trees, CO_2 is sequestered throughout the lifetime of the tree from which it is harvested. Cork typically has a thermal conductivity in the region of 0.038–0.050 W/m°C. The main use for cork in building is for insulating flat roofs using a method known as warm roof construction, that is where the insulation is towards the outside of the roof build up, normally directly below the waterproof membrane and thus keeping the roof 'warm'. Cork is a waterproof material and is naturally resistant to most pests (with the exception of wasps) because of naturally occurring formaldehyde. Cork is a dimensionally stable material, has a fairly high compressive strength, and can be supplied in boards of differing thicknesses which can be pre-cut to create a fall on an otherwise flat roof. Other advantages include being a renewable resource, being reusable and also being recyclable as a loose fill insulation material. Disadvantages include: its high-embodied energy; the dust created when cutting may be a health hazard; and wet cork can harbour mould growth (the spores of which may cause an allergic reaction). There may also be a small amount of emission into the atmosphere of the naturally occurring formaldehyde.

Openings
Every time there is an opening placed in the building envelope for a window or door, the insulation levels

tend to be compromised and cold bridging tends to occur. A cold bridge occurs where the arrangement of materials or components create a heat path that makes it easy for heat to escape through the building envelope. Take a window opening, for example: all the way around the outside edge of the window opening (be it at the head at the top of the window, the cill at the bottom or the window reveals at the sides) the harder materials that conduct heat easily tend to interrupt the line of insulation. The window frame itself tends to be so much thinner than the wall that it cannot possibly be as well insulated. Then there is the glass itself, a hard dense material that is very good at conducting heat. Taking into consideration the fact that windows can make up 20 or 30 per cent or more of the surface area of the external walls, then there is significant potential heat loss

through windows and so it is important to consider how to improve the performance of each aspect in turn.

Firstly, ensure that cold bridging is eliminated around openings by making sure that the insulation layer is not compromised.

Secondly, choose a frame material that minimizes heat loss. The two best readily available window frame materials are PVC and wood. Wood is a reasonably good insulator but still presents an uninterrupted heat path to the outside. Insulated frames are available that have insulation sandwiched between layers of wood, but these tend to be rather expensive and have not yet received the test of time. The main drawback with wood is that it is a maintenance issue. PVC windows perform as well as wood framed windows but are not as environmentally

Rigid board insulation is generally not as airtight as batt insulation due to gaps at edges.

Openings are one potential weakness in maintaining an effective air barrier.

friendly in that there are a number of pollutants released in their manufacture.

Thirdly and most importantly the largest difference can be made by choosing a high performance insulated glazing unit (IGU). Glazing technology has moved on in leaps and bounds over the last number of years, and it is now possible to buy insulated glazing units that have the same insulation value as a wall. Technologies commonly employed now include double, triple and quadruple glazed units with the spaces between the panes filled with inert gases such as argon or xenon, and the surfaces of the glass coated with a low-emissivity (low-e) coating (a low-e coating has roughly the same effect as adding an additional pane of glass). If your budget is tight, then you will need to be strategic with respect to what you will spend your money on. It is good practice to place higher performing IGUs to the north where there is less solar gain, place slightly lower-performing IGUs to the south where the south-facing glazing will be admitting free heat gains, with a view to achieving an overall net gain in heat transfer.

Air Tightness and Ventilation

All new houses built in the UK and Ireland are required to achieve a certain level of air-tightness to meet the current Building Regulations.

In the UK and Ireland it is $10m^3/hr/m^2$ (Part L Building Regulations). This regulation is designed to prevent unwanted and uncontrolled heat loss through air leaks in the building envelope and is a worthwhile goal. Houses that are well built can achieve 0.6 ACH at 50 Pascals, which is the very high standard achieved by the German Passive House Company, but this takes a lot of attention to detail and exemplary construction methods to achieve. Unless the form of the house is very simple, it will be difficult to achieve very high levels of air tightness. The way in which air tightness is tested is to have a blower door test carried out when the house is sealed. A blower door test uses a large fan with a known airflow placed across and fully enclosing an external opening such as a door and works by temporarily lowering the air pressure in the house. This has the effect of increasing the flow of air through any leaks in the structure, which is measured against the known airflow of the fan. This is a very useful test to have carried out, not so much to prove to building control that your house meets the minimum standard, but to prove to yourself that the house has indeed been well sealed and if not to identify where the weaknesses are and to eliminate or minimize their effect.

Even with 0.6 ACH, rooms will become unpleasant if there is a lot of activity and a lot of moisture being generated in them. Did you know for example that as you sleep you release one litre of water into the bedroom in the form of water vapour? The traditional way of dealing with ventilation is to open a window when things get a bit stuffy or, if you are a rugged type, you may have your windows open all of the time. The building regulations deal with the issue by stipulating a certain size of operable window and permavents which in most cases can be closed off altogether. Ventilation is one of the often overlooked aspects of building a house. As houses have become better insulated, they have also become more airtight both by regulation and through new methods of construction, and in the process ventilation has become even more important so it cannot simply be left to chance. We need to breathe fresh air to keep healthy, but what we do not want to do is to leave windows open all year round to do so. The reason is obvious; any heat that is in the house will be displaced by cold air from outside. How then do we overcome the challenge of achieving good ventilation

Inverter for converting DC current from PV panel to AC current.

rates, and at the same time keeping the house warm, particularly in winter?

There are many solutions to the challenge of achieving adequate ventilation, but these boil down to two main methods; passive ventilation and active ventilation.

Passive ventilation

Passive ventilation uses the forces of natural air movement such as the wind or buoyancy forces caused by warm air to provide the required ventilation. The simplest form of passive ventilation is to have holes in the building fabric, but because there is no control over the level of ventilation, this is impractical. The most common method of achieving passive ventilation is to have operable windows. The advantages of this method include being able to control the level of ventilation and that the windows then serve more than one function. The disadvantage is that the incoming air is probably at a lower temperature than that required internally. An alternative method is to use passive ventilators but once again, the incoming air will only be at ambient temperature. The solution

to this issue is to use ventilators that incorporate a method of heat recovery. The main disadvantage is that there may be insufficient ventilation in very still conditions. In such circumstances a fan may be required as a backup to move sufficient air. When fans are used the system becomes active ventilation.

Active ventilation

Active ventilation uses fans to move the air. This can be as simple as having extractor fans or fans that pressurize the interior. To be considered energy efficient the fans should use less than one watt per litre of air moved. For super-insulated dwellings, a whole house ventilation system with heat recovery is normally used. The most efficient systems use two low energy fans, one for intake air and the other for exhaust air. The incoming and exhaust air both pass through the heat exchanger and the outgoing warm air heats the heat exchanger which in turn heats the incoming air to almost room temperature. Having gone to the trouble of installing a whole house ventilation system with heat recovery, it makes sense to utilize this to provide space heating when it is required. This can be achieved by placing a heater unit in the intake air supply. The heater unit can be supplied from the solar water heated thermal store, and backed up by a heat pump or other energy source if necessary. It is the integration of each of the systems that achieves the overall efficiency. Remember that each system is doing more than one thing.

Free Energy

Now that we have established the principle of insulation first, free energy second, we need to examine where this energy will come from and before we even consider using renewable energy sources, we need to consider just how much energy is needed, and what it is needed for. At the most basic level we need energy for space heating, water heating, cooking and lighting but of course we have come to rely on many other electrically powered luxuries in life that we now regard as necessities.

When many people think about free energy today, they think about wind turbines or solar photovoltaic panels producing electricity, whereas some others may think of ground sourced heat pumps and under-floor heating; the list is almost endless. What should come to mind before anything else is the free energy we get from the sun. Now, if you live in an area that is not blessed with too many hours of direct sunshine throughout the year, the single most important energy source for you is still the sun. It is the sun's energy that the earth receives that drives the climate and weather systems on planet earth. The sun provides us with energy in the form of light and in doing so it also provides us with heat. Even on a cloudy day the sun's energy penetrates the cloud but is dispersed to provide diffused sunlight which is still an effective form of energy. It is this source of free energy that you want to be able to utilize in your sustainable house.

Incidental Heat Gains

There are a number of other sources of free heat that need to be taken into consideration when designing a house. Each of these heat sources is quite small in comparison to the energy available from the sun, but the cumulative effect of each of the items can be significant. For example, each person within the house emits heat on a constant basis, and the higher a person's metabolism, the greater the amount of heat emitted. Every electrical item within a house emits heat and the larger the number of these the greater will be the heat gains. It could be argued that these gains from electrical appliances are not actually free (hence the title; incidental heat gains) because one still has to purchase the electricity that is being consumed by the appliance, but what we are considering here is free heat. A fridge is used for keeping food cold so we purchase electricity for the fridge to do its job. In the process however it produces heat; this is the free heat we are referring to. It is particularly important to take free heat gains into consideration when the envelope of your house is very well insulated because the heating system will only be required to make up the difference between the total fabric heat loss and the cumulative total of all of the available free heat gains. There is a substantial amount of heat released during cooking and in a very well insulated house may cause overheating unless the heat can be redistributed to another part of the house. Given the fact that it is a requirement of the building regulations that there is an extractor fan in the kitchen, one could argue that the heat can simply be dumped using the extractor fan, however this defeats the purpose of trying to create a low energy house. Better to use some form of heat exchanger to recover the heat from the stale ventilation air that is to be dumped and redistribute the pre-warmed clean fresh air to another part of the house.

One of the largest sources of incidental gains can be utilized by locating the heating and hot water systems, including all of the pipe-work, entirely within the insulated building envelope, where all the heat losses from these elements then become heat gains.

Energy Storage

Having first considered the importance of insulating the building envelope, and allowing free energy from the sun to get inside the building envelope second, it is now time to consider energy storage. One of the challenges presented with passive solar design is that often the time that we need heat from the sun most is at night time when it is not available or during the winter when the strength of the sun is at its lowest.

Structural opening for novel hot water thermal store in the form of a lap pool.

To make use of heat gains when they are available we not only need to be able to collect the energy but we also need to be able to store the heat so that it can be used later in the day when it is required. Heat can be stored in the floors, walls and ceilings and thankfully most forms of traditional construction used in the British Isles will provide a reasonable amount of thermal storage. Traditional masonry cavity wall construction provides ample such storage for excess heat, but it has one major drawback. The usual way to provide insulation in a cavity wall is to place the insulation within the cavity; however the thickness of insulation is limited by the cavity width. Increasing the cavity width is possible using a solution that is specifically engineer-designed and that utilizes non-conventional cavity wall ties. Bear in mind that if you go down this route the foundation widths will increase, and if you are building on a tight site, the increase in wall thickness may limit the internal size

of your house to such a degree that it becomes impractical. The normal way to increase the insulation value of a masonry cavity wall is to use an aerated concrete block inner leaf or to add an additional layer of insulation to the inside of the inner leaf. Unfortunately this has the effect of insulating the thermal mass from air in the room, thus rendering it ineffective as a heat store. It is much easier to achieve high levels of insulation using timber frame construction than traditional masonry construction because a simple increase in frame size allows for an increase in insulation thickness, but heat storage is a little more challenging. Heat can be stored in heavyweight floor slabs or in hot water.

BUILDING SERVICES

The term building services refers to any electrical or mechanical installations within buildings including

Over-sized thermal hot water store to store hot water from solar water panels.

heating, hot and cold water, ventilation and electrical circuits and lighting. From a sustainable design point of view it is vital that the building services are fully integrated into the design so that they complement the overall design strategy.

Space Heating and Hot Water

If your house is insulated properly then there should only be a minimal requirement for space heating. Furthermore, if you have designed the house to make maximum use of solar energy, then this again will

89

reduce the requirement for supplementary heating. It may even be possible to do away with heating altogether if you are happy to put up with cooler internal temperatures, but remember that the World Health Organisation's (WHO) recommendation for indoor temperature is 18°C and that for the elderly, young and handicapped, the recommended temperature is two to three degrees warmer. In prolonged periods of cold temperatures with minimal sunshine, even with a super-insulated house, temperatures can fall below the WHO's recommendation. This means that you will more than likely require some form of supplementary heating for cold spells. In a poorly insulated house, traditional central heating generally supplies heat to large radiators in each room. In a super insulated house, only minimal heating will be required in each room and in the house as a whole. This means that a traditional heating system will be vastly oversized and therefore inefficient and underused. It also means that you can consider using alternative energy sources that would not be viable in a conventional house. It is possible with careful design to utilize passive solar design as the primary source of heating; then use the hot water produced by solar water heaters to provide auxiliary space heating and, only when there is insufficient heating from solar energy, an alternative energy source can provide the minimal back-up required.

Traditional Boilers

If you insist on using a traditional boiler system then at the very minimum you will need to use a condensing boiler as they are more efficient than non-condensing boilers. In order to utilize the boiler in an efficient manner however, it should be coupled to a thermal water store so that the boiler can work on full load when heat input is required. The thermal store should be large enough to allow significant quantities of heat to be extracted from it so that the boiler does not need to fire again for some time. This will cut out the highly inefficient boiler cycling associated with traditional boiler systems. The hot water thus produced can be used for domestic hot water and for space heating.

Wood Fired Boilers

Since wood sequestrates carbon as it grows, is a renewable resource and is in plentiful supply, then using a wood-fired boiler rather than a traditional gas or oil boiler makes ecological sense.

Their sustainability credentials include being highly efficient and, along with a wide choice of designs, this has led to a recent rise in their popularity. They operate just like a conventional boiler with wood pellets or chips being fed from a hopper. Despite their high capital cost, they are the boiler of choice for sustainable dwellings. Their high initial cost and the space required for fuel storage are their main drawbacks, and the cleaning out and maintenance can become an issue as occupants get older.

Wood/Multi-fuel Stoves

Much like wood fired boilers, modern multi-fuel stoves are efficient and can contribute to low overall energy consumption. Their main benefit is in not having to be dependent on one fuel source.

Wood-fired boiler in the Kingspan Lighthouse.

Flat plate collector and integrated thermal store.

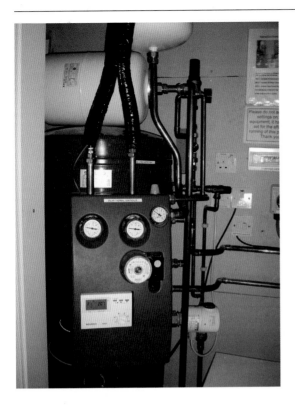

Hanson EcoHouse ground source heat pump thermal hot water store.

Ground/Water/Air Source Heat Pumps

Heat can be extracted from the ground, water or air using a heat pump and because of the efficiencies involved it is considered to be a renewable resource. The main drawback is that the heat pump requires electricity to run.

Solar Water Heaters

Solar water heaters come in a variety of shapes and sizes. They are categorized by the collector type and method of water storage. Collector types include: concentrating collectors, through evacuated tube collectors, to flat plate collectors. Storage vessels can be integrated with the collector or remote from the collector.

The two types most commonly used in dwellings in the UK and Ireland are flat plate collectors and evacuated tube collectors. Evacuated tube collectors have a slightly higher capital cost but they are more efficient than flat plate collectors and collect useful solar energy even in overcast conditions.

In a super insulated house, by using a slightly larger array of evacuated tube collectors connected to a larger than normal thermal water store, sufficient energy can be stored to supply a significant portion of both domestic hot water and space heating needs.

Ventilation

Ventilation has already been dealt with previously in

Ground source heat pump in the Hanson EcoHouse at the BRE Innovation Park.

Evacuated tube solar water heating array.

the chapter, but if mechanical ventilation with heat recovery is being considered for your house then it would normally come under the general description of building services. If you are employing the services of a Building Services Engineer then ensure that the engineer is fully conversant with the whole rationale behind the design and remember that ventilation needs to be designed as part of the overall house package.

Electricity Production

One of the difficulties in using electricity as supplied by the public electricity service providers is that the majority of this electricity is produced by burning fossil fuels which of course not only uses up finite resources but also produces large quantities of CO_2. There are, however, a number of methods of producing your own electricity including: micro-hydro where electricity is generated from running

water; wind power where electricity is generated from the wind; and photovoltaic panels that generate electricity from sunlight. If your budget will stretch to any of the above methods you should endeavour to incorporate them in your design. At the date of writing there were grants available to help offset the installation costs associated with these renewable electricity technologies.

Lighting

Having designed your house to utilize as much daylight as possible, you will require some form of artificial lighting for when daylight is not available. You should use only low energy light fittings both internally and externally and there is now an excellent range of light fittings to choose from. The majority of low energy light fittings utilize fluorescent lamps, but LED technology has improved to such an extent that these are a viable alternative. Do

Solar photovoltaic panel beside evacuated tube collector.

not be afraid of using the services of a lighting professional to design the lighting. They will be able to advise you of the latest fittings available and can source fittings that are not on display at your local lighting shop.

Electrical Appliances

In order to use as little energy as possible, you should use only electrical equipment that has a high energy efficiency rating. Ratings range from A–G, with A being the most efficient and G being the least efficient.

Controls

The importance of having good controls on all passive systems and mechanical and electrical services

cannot be emphasized enough. There is little point in having a house with a thermally efficient building envelope and having little or no control of how or when the environmental control systems operate. In a fully passive building the simplest forms of control may suffice, for example you can manually operate the various systems within your house, such as opening a window for ventilation or switching on a heater for additional heat when required. This is all well and good if you are prepared to be diligent as to how and when these control devices are used. Mostly however, householders are too busy to continually monitor and control their indoor environment and resort to some form of automation using an automatic control.

Modern controls range from simple thermostatic

3 Zone 24/7 space and hot water heating controller.

valves on heating systems to whole building management systems that monitor the existing internal and external conditions and adjust the settings on the mechanical and electrical services accordingly. The degree of control required will be determined by the systems incorporated in your house. Adequate control of each system is required but of equal importance is ease of use. A system that can do everything is useless if you do not know how to use it. Insist on ease of use when determining control systems for your house.

Water

The majority of houses within the UK and Ireland obtain water from public water service providers. As the population has grown, and as more and more houses have been built, the demands on the existing infrastructure have increased correspondingly. In recent years water shortages and the now widespread use of water meters has risen to some prominence in the media and there are calls to conserve water. Some have argued that there is no scarcity of water in the British Isles, so why try to conserve it? What this argument fails to recognize is the cost of providing water both in financial and energy terms. It is evident that the cost of providing potable water is increasing, and increasingly the consumer has to pay for the water used. For this argument alone it is worth conserving water, but above and beyond this, the vast quantity of energy used to deliver clean water provides an even stronger and compelling argument to conserve this precious resource.

Energy Efficiency Checklist

Have you considered the following aspects of site layout?
- Access to solar radiation and daylight.
- Shelter from the wind.
- Building orientation.
- Choice of external materials.

Have you considered the following aspects of the building envelope?
- Building form.
- Building fabric.
- Insulation.

- Air tightness.
- Free energy.
- Storage for excess free energy.

Have you considered the following aspects of the proposed building services?
- Heating and hot water.
- Ventilation.
- Lighting.
- Electrical appliances.
- Controls.

CONCLUSION

Chapter Seven has emphasized the importance of designing for energy efficiency including site layout, the building envelope and the services to be installed in the house. At every opportunity, the use of free energy should be optimized by insulation, admitting and storing free energy gains such as solar energy. All building services should also be designed to be as energy efficient as possible, should respond quickly to changing environmental conditions and should be capable of being controlled automatically to reduce energy consumption.

CHAPTER EIGHT

Building Regulations

Chapter Eight provides an overview of the Building Regulations and emphasizes that Part L (England and Wales and the Republic of Ireland) of the Building Regulations presents minimum statutory requirements only for the conservation of fuel and power. It compares the energy use of a house that just complies with the building regulations to a house designed with energy efficiency in mind.

Using the Building Regulations

Professionals who use the Building Regulations on a daily basis should know just where to find each aspect of the regulations that is applicable to the building they are dealing with. Not only that, but they should also know what particular regulations insist on and will incorporate any relevant aspects into the design at an early stage. If you are not in the building trade or professions, then more than likely you will not have such an in-depth knowledge and the task of ensuring compliance may look a little daunting. Just to make matters a little more difficult, some sustainable construction techniques are not mainstream enough to be even mentioned in the regulations. Since this is likely to be the case with your house, then set up a meeting at the earliest opportunity with your local building control officer and discuss your proposals to ensure that in principle they will meet their minimum standards. What follows in this chapter is an overview of what the regulations are, what they set out to achieve, and an outline of the various sections. Only those regulations that have an impact on the early design stages are covered and even then, not in every detail. Particular attention is paid to the conservation of fuel and power and other regulations that relate in some way to sustainable construction.

What are the Building Regulations?

Building Regulations are legal requirements (referred to as Schedules in England and Wales) that are aimed at achieving minimum standards of building work for the construction of buildings. Please note that they are minimum standards only that every building has to meet, but if you are serious about building a sustainable house then you will want to surpass a number of the standards particularly in connection with how much energy your house is likely to use. Building Regulations set out the definitions of what is regarded as 'building work' and the procedures for ensuring that building work meets the standards laid down. In the UK, Building Regulations are laid down by Acts of Parliament and are supported by separate documents containing practical and technical guidance on compliance, which are known as 'Approved Documents' (in England and Wales). It is the approved documents that are referred to most when seeking technical advice on the standards.

The main purpose of Building Regulations is to ensure the health and safety of persons in or around buildings, to conserve fuel and power, and to provide facilities and access for the disabled. Building regulations are administered by the Building Control Departments of local authorities.

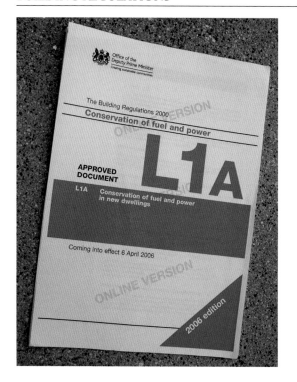

Building Regulations Part L1A – Conservation of Fuel and Power (England and Wales).

In England and Wales in total there are 14 Parts (A-H and J-N) to these requirements. They cover subjects such as structure, fire safety, ventilation, drainage, energy conservation, and access and facilities for all including disabled people. The requirements are performance based, that is they are expressed in broad, functional terms in order to give designers and builders the maximum flexibility in the design and construction stages of building.

In Scotland there are seven parts to the regulations, Part 0 deals with General Matters, part 1 Structure, Part 2 Fire, Part 3 Environment, Part 4 Safety, Part 5 Noise, and Part 6 Energy.

It is important to use the latest versions of the Building Regulations so check the following websites for up to date publications:

http://www.sbsa.gov.uk/tech_handbooks/th_pdf_2008/domestic/Domestic.pdf

http://www.buildingcontrol-ni.com/site/default.asp?secid=home

http://www.sbsa.gov.uk/index.htm

http://www.communities.gov.uk/planningandbuilding/buildingregulations/legislation/england-wales/

http://www.environ.ie/en/

Each of the Approved Documents deals with a particular aspect of the Building Regulations, but compliance with that aspect does not necessarily mean that you will comply with another aspect. It is therefore worth checking in the notes section at the beginning of each Approved Document for references to other Approved Documents that also apply; for example in the Notes section of Part M – Access to and Use of Buildings, reference is also made to Approved Document B – Fire Safety in connection with Means of Escape in Case of Fire, Approved Document K – Protection from Falling, Collision and Impact, in

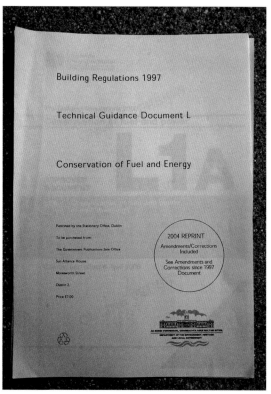

Technical Guidance Document L – Conservation of Fuel and Energy (Ireland).

Equivalent Regulations for England, Wales, Northern Ireland, Scotland and the Republic of Ireland

	England and Wales	Northern Ireland	Scotland	Republic of Ireland
General –	Regulation 7	Part A	Part 0	
Materials and Workmanship		Part B		
Toxic Substances	Part D			
Site Preparation and Resistance to Moisture	Part C	Part C	Part 3	Part C
Structure	Part A	Part D	Part 1	Part A
Fire Safety	Part B	Part E	Part 2	Part B
Conservation of Fuel and Power	Part L	Part F	Part 6	Part L
Sound	Part E	Part G	Part 5	Part E
Stairs, Ramps, Guarding and Protection from Impact	Part M	Part H	Part 4	Part K
Hygiene	Part G			
Electrical Safety	Part P			
Ventilation	Part F	Part K	Part 3	Part F
Heat Producing Appliances		Part L	Part 3	Part J
Drainage	Part H	Part N	Part 3	Part H
Unventilated Hot Water Storage Systems		Part P	Part 4.9	
Access and Facilities for Disabled People	Part M	Part R	Part 4	Part M
Glazing	Part N	Part V	Part 4	Part D

Continuity of the air barrier requires careful design and sequential installation.

If tubular fluorescent lamps are used, T8 (26mm tube diameter) lamps, or preferably T5 (16mm diameter) lamps should be specified.

Fixed External Lighting
Fixed external lighting must:

(a) have a maximum output of 150W per fitting and automatically switch off:
   (i) when there is adequate daylight; and
   (ii) when not required at night;
or
(b) have sockets that can only be fitted with lamps having a luminous efficacy greater than 40 lumens per circuit-Watt.

It should be noted that fluorescent and dedicated compact fluorescent light fittings would meet this requirement, but those accommodating GLS tungsten lamps and compact fluorescent lamps with a bayonet cap or Edison screw base, or tungsten halogen lamps would not.

The table on page 104 is the checklist for Criterion 2 as given in the approved documents.

Criterion 3 – Limiting the effects of solar gains

This clause states that provisions should be made to limit internal temperatures due to excessive solar gains. This is standard practice when designing a low-energy, passive solar dwelling. It can be achieved by an appropriate combination of window size and orientation, solar protection by shading or other solar control measures, ventilation (day and night) and high thermal capacity.

The regulation rightly mentions that adequate provision should be made for day-lighting when trying to limit solar gains. In thermally lightweight houses the surfaces on which the sun (and thus heat) falls directly should be as light and reflective as possible to allow the light to be distributed throughout the space to be absorbed by as large a surface area as possible. If the surface on which the sun falls directly is a thermally heavyweight material then a dark and non-reflective surface will better absorb and store the heat.

Criterion 4 – Quality of design, construction and commissioning

This criterion relates specifically to the thermal and air permeability properties of the building envelope, and the building services and controls.

Air permeability
The building regulations require a maximum permissible air permeability of $10m^3/(hr.m^2)@50Pa$ to be confirmed after construction (but prior to completion) by a pressure test carried out in accordance with the procedure set out in the ATTMA publication *Measuring air permeability of building envelopes*. For a house to achieve Code 6 this figure will be required to be less than $3m^3/(hr.m^2)@50Pa$ and a target figure of $0.6m^3/(hr.m^2)@50Pa$ should be set.

Pressure Testing
It is likely that your house will not be built using the accredited construction details as provided by Building Control. If this is the case than you will be required to have your house pressure tested to determine the air permeability.

Building Fabric
The Building Regulations require that the building fabric be constructed such that there are no readily avoidable thermal bridges in the insulation layers caused by gaps within the various elements, at joints between elements, and at the edges of elements such as those around door and window openings. This is good practice for low energy design and every attempt should be made to avoid or minimize thermal bridges at every opportunity.

Criterion 5 – Operating and maintenance instructions
Operating and maintenance instructions
You or your builder should provide clear and simple operating and maintenance instructions for both fixed building services and the dwelling as a whole to help ensure the services can be operated and maintained in an energy efficient manner. Examples of the kind of information to include are: how to adjust the time and temperature settings of heating controls and how to maintain services and any equipment included with the home at optimum energy efficiency.

Criterion 2 – Minimum acceptable standards

No	Check	Evidence	Produced by	Design compliant?	As built compliant?
	U-values				
6	Are all U-values within the minimum acceptable?	Schedule of U-values output by calculation software	SAP assessment		
	Common areas in building with multiple dwellings				
7	If the common areas are unheated, are all U-values within the design limits given in the table on page 101?	Schedule of U-values output by calculation software			
	Heating and hot water systems				
8	Does the efficiency of the heating systems meet the minimum values given in *The Domestic Heating Compliance Guide?*	Schedule of appliances efficiencies output by calculation software	SAP assessment		
9	Does the insulation of the hot water cylinder meet the standards given in *The Domestic Heating Compliance Guide?*	Cylinder insulation specification as output by calculation software			
10	Do the controls meet the minimum provisions given in *The Domestic Heating Compliance Guide?*	Controls specification as output from calculation software	SAP assessment		
11	Does the heating and hot water system meet the other minimum provisions given in *The Domestic Heating Compliance Guide?*	Schedule of compliance provisions as output from calculation software	Builder or heating engineer		
	Fixed internal and external lighting				
12	Does the fixed internal lighting comply with paras 2.34 to 2.36?	Schedule of fixed internal lighting	Builder or electrical contractor		
13	Does the fixed external lighting comply with paras 2.37 to 2.38?	Schedule of fixed external lighting	Builder or electrical contractor		

The Energy Rating of your Home

The Building Regulations require that an energy rating be calculated for your house as built and a notice stating the energy rating be fixed in the dwelling.

OPERATIONS ON SITE

When it comes to operations on site you will have to notify building control before some work sections are started or immediately after some sections of work are completed.

Stages of the work that which require specific notification are:

- Commencement of work
- Excavations for foundations
- Foundation concrete (poured)
- Materials laid over a site (damp-proof membrane and sub-floor make-up) before concrete poured
- Drains before they are covered up
- Drains after they are covered up (backfilled and ready for testing)
- Occupation (only relevant if part of the building is to be occupied, for example a flat)
- Completion

Other stages that Building Control need to know about are:

'First fix' or 'pre-plaster', before electrical wiring, structural elements such as lintels and beams and insulation materials concealed in walls, floors or roof spaces are covered by render, plaster or plasterboard. It is desirable, but not mandatory, that building control is notified before floor joists or roof construction is covered up so that these elements can be inspected if time permits.

Completion

In Scotland the Completion Certificate Submission form is supplied to the applicant along with the Building Warrant to be filled in by the applicant. When the building works are finished, the form is completed and returned to the Building Standards Section for approval. It is important that you submit the Completion Certificate only when you are completely satisfied that you have carried out all works in

Inform Building Control before covering up pipe and cable runs.

conformity with your Building Warrant. If for any reason you have carried out additional works that require Building Control approval, then assuming that the work has been carried out in accord with the Building Standards, then this work should be described in writing and in drawn format and submitted to Building Control so that it too can be approved. Before Building Control accepts the Completion Certificate, a Building Standards Officer will inspect the work that you have carried out to confirm that it is in general accord with the Building Warrant and that the Building Regulations have been complied with.

Where electrical work has been carried out an Electrical Certificate should also be completed by your electrician and submitted along with your Completion Certificate. The local authority must take reasonable steps to satisfy itself that the electrical works have been designed, installed, inspected and tested in accordance with BS 7671: 2001 (Requirements for Electrical Installations) to ensure compliance with the Building Standards. Guidance issued by the Scottish Building Standards Agency (SBSA) to verifiers states:

On submitting a Completion Certificate to the Verifier the relevant person submitting the Completion Certificate should also provide:-

1. A Certificate of Construction*, or

2. a relevant BS 7671 Certificate, together with inspection and test results, completed and signed by a competent person**

where;

* A Certificate of Construction is a certificate issued by an Approved Certifier of Construction. A register of Approved Certifiers can be found on the Scottish Building Standards Agency website www.sbsa.gov.uk. It should also be noted that a refund may be issued where a verifier has been informed of the intention to use an approved certifier of construction on the prescribed form prior to the works being carried out.

and

** A competent person is deemed to be an installer having current membership of a UKAS accredited registration scheme operated by NICEIC or SELECT or an equivalent body.

This means that the electrical installations are to be certified by a competent person either through the Approved Certification of Construction Scheme (ACC) or in accordance with the relevant BS7671 with associated schedules of inspections, test results and so on. The relevant certificates are considered as an electrical installation certificate, minor electrical certificate or periodic inspection report and should be issued dependent on the type of electrical work involved. It is worth noting that Building Control will not accept the submission of a BS7671 Certificate completed and signed by any other person other than a competent person.

Building Control must confirm the acceptance of the Completion Certificate in writing before you may use or occupy the building. This is important for insurances and other legal reasons. All papers relating to the Building Warrant and to the acceptance of your Completion Certificate are important documents and should be retained with your Title Deeds as they will be required should you sell your property.

CONCLUSION

Every aspect of your house must comply with the relevant building regulation but for an energy efficient and sustainable house, you will want to exceed the requirements of the regulations dealing with energy use in particular.

Finance, Tenders and Contracts

Chapter Nine provides an overview of how to deal with building finances, the tendering process and standard building contracts that are suitable for particular projects.

FINANCE

Setting your budget

One of the first industries to feel the effects of a recession is the building industry. When the economy is doing well, the building industry booms, but as soon as there is a downturn, things change. Just before the credit crunch really began to bite in 2008, it was relatively easy to raise finance for a self-build project. Lenders were very welcoming to anyone wanting to build their own home. In fact for a long time it was easily possible to borrow up to 95 per cent of land and building costs and it was possible to receive cash payments up front before each of the building project stages. This was of great help to the self-builder and the resulting cash-flow in many instances allowed the self builder to stay in their own home while their new home was being built. To qualify for a loan some lenders only required that a plot have outline planning permission, others required full planning permission and building control approval before they would lend. Things changed dramatically however within a short period of time. Some of the banks got into difficulties and governments had to step in to bail them out. One of the reasons cited for banks getting into such a pickle was that they were lending too much money for property. Almost overnight it became very difficult to borrow money to purchase property or build, and as a result the property market entered a period of stagnation. As in the past, when recovery occurs and as confidence grows in the financial world, then lenders should begin to lend again. For a period of time, banks will be very cautious about lending for self build projects.

In calculating your budget for your new build project you need to take a realistic view of how much money is available to you and how much money you will have to spend. If you are in the very fortunate position of having enough cash to build exactly what you want, then you do not need to worry about where the money will come from. For most people though, building a new house will mean having to borrow at least some of the money required. For some, the building costs will be paid for by the sale of existing property, but even then, money may need to be borrowed for a short period of time until the existing house is sold. If the housing market is in stagnation then it may be years before you are able to sell your own property. The traditional method of calculating the maximum sum that a lender is willing to advance for a mortgage is based on ability to repay the loan. This is normally calculated in multiples of the income of the people who will be repaying the loan. Cautious lenders will want a substantial deposit and will only lend two to three times the value of the principal income. Other less cautious lenders will require only a small deposit and will stretch to upwards of four times the combined household income. It always pays off to shop around. Do not only approach the high street lenders. There are many reputable mortgage brokers who know the market and who can shop around to get the best deal for your circumstances.

You may have a good idea as to how much you can afford to spend on your house, but it is always wise at the outset of the project to take independent financial advice from your accountant or other financial professional so that you can establish just how much you can afford. You need to be honest in relation to all of your outgoings; both short and long term financial commitments, and try also to anticipate any additional expenditure that you may need to commit to in the near future. You should use this figure to establish your budget during the feasibility stage at the outset of the project and with good project management you should be able to build your house within your budget. As the saying goes, you will just have to cut your cloth to suit. It goes without saying that the budget you set yourself must be realistic. There is little point in setting yourself a budget that you cannot afford, neither is there any point in setting yourself a budget that will not allow you to build the house that you have set your sights on.

Your overall budget needs to take into account financial costs, site costs, design costs, statutory fees, setting up costs, building costs, VAT and other taxes and a contingency sum for unforeseen circumstances. When setting your initial budget it is important to recognize that unforeseen problems can (and will) arise at any stage throughout the design and building process, which may have significant financial implications. Because of this, traditional building contracts have a contingency sum built into the overall contract value. This sum is normally in the order of some 10 per cent of the total contract value and is only used at the discretion of the architect or whoever else is administering the contract. For a self-build project the amount of contingency should be increased to 15 to 20 per cent of the overall budget unless of course you are very experienced at the self-build game. Most importantly remember that cash flow is vital to the success of any project so you need to ensure that the funding you require will be available at the various times you will need it throughout the design and build process.

There are a number of ways of raising the funding to finance your project. The majority of people considering building will have a house to sell and the equity in their existing house will cover at least some of the cost of building. If you choose to sell your house you will need to consider the cost of renting a property or hiring a mobile home for the duration of the project. You may also need to factor in the costs associated with storage of your furniture and other personal effects.

Finance Costs

The majority of people seeking to build for themselves will require some form of finance. When purchasing a house built already, this finance would normally take the form of a mortgage, where the lending institution would lend against the security of the value of the existing property. With a self-build project, however, as yet there is no security to lend against other than the value of the land and the projected value of the finished project so a self-build mortgage is what most self-builders use to finance their project. In times of economic uncertainty, the lending institutions may well place a very low value on the finished project, compounding the difficulty in raising sufficient finance for your project.

Self-Build Mortgage

To a large extent, self-build mortgages tend to have similar terms and conditions to conventional mortgages. In addition, repayment and interest-only mortgages are available along with the usual offerings of fixed, capped, and variable interest rates. There are, however, two main differences between self-build mortgages and conventional mortgages. Firstly, for self-build mortgages the maximum loan-to-value is normally no more than 75 per cent of the total cost, whereas conventional domestic mortgages range upwards from 75 per cent. Secondly, with self-build mortgages the funds are released in stages instead of all at once.

Since the recent financial crash, self-build mortgage providers will want to reduce the risk of lending as far as possible. They will base their decision to lend on a variety of factors related to the project and to you. If you are applying for a self-build mortgage you will be more successful if you approach prospective lenders with confidence and having all of the required information to hand. The information they will be looking for will include:

- A copy of the planning permission approval and approved drawings for your house.
- A copy of the detailed design drawings and detailed specification for your house.
- A copy of your Building Control Approval and the Building Control Drawings.
- A detailed cost breakdown for the house showing costs for each works package.
- A detailed construction programme with a realistic completion date of around six to twelve months.
- Copies of all the relevant insurances or if you are using a builder, confirmation that they have the necessary insurances.
- A copy of your architect's or building surveyor's professional indemnity insurance to cover the issue of certificates.

- Details of any relevant structural or building warranty scheme.

There is a further problem facing self-builders in that often they have to continue to finance their existing home while building their new home. If you borrow money it is going to cost. Just how much it costs depends on how much you borrow, at what interest rate and for how long. Obviously the less you borrow, the less you will have to pay back in interest, equally the lower the interest rates the less you will have to pay back, and if you project manage the whole process in an efficient manner and build in as short a time as possible, then again you will pay less for financing the project.

The stages for release of funds for self-build mortgages depend to a large extent on the mortgage provider. Traditionally the stages were up to foundations, wind and watertight and then on to completion. More recently additional stages were added to

Carry out a thorough site analysis prior to purchasing your site.

help with cash flow. For masonry construction staged payments are at: purchase of site; foundations and preliminary costs; wall plate level; wind and watertight; first fix and plastered out; and second fix through to completion. For a timber-frame house the stages are: purchase of site; preliminary costs and foundations to base plate; timber frame erected, wind and watertight; first fix and dry lined; and second fix through to completion.

Site Costs

The purchase of your site along with the associated professional and stamp duty fees will be your first major item of expense. As a rule of thumb, you should budget to spend approximately one-third of your money on the site, one-third on building materials, and one-third on labour. It is always recommended to carry out a thorough analysis of the site prior to purchase to ensure that your proposals are actually feasible and that you can build the house you want within your budget.

Design Costs

Spending money on quality professional services for a good design for your new home is money well spent. You should ensure that your architect is briefed properly and only use an architect who has experience in low energy and sustainable design. It is also worthwhile to employ the services of a quantity surveyor to provide you with budget costs throughout the design process. Once again, you should employ only those who have experience in sustainable design and the self-build market to ensure that the budget costs are realistic. The greatest benefit of employing a quantity surveyor in the early stages of the design process is that they can advise you at an early stage of the realistic size of house your that budget will stretch to, and then throughout the design process they can keep an eye on the design to ensure that it can be built within budget. For contentious sites where there are likely to be problems with obtaining planning permission you may need to budget for the services of other professionals such as a planning consultant or a roads engineer. Your architect should be able to advise you of the requirement for such services. Design team fees may seem expensive, but if your design saves you time and money and provides

you with the sustainable house you desire, then in the long run the initial cost of your design team is worth it. You will require detailed planning permission and at the very least have applied for building control approval prior to commencing building work on site. If you are proposing to incorporate specialist renewable energy technologies in your design, then ensure that the cost of designing these is included in the overall design team fee, or if not, ensure that you obtain these from specialist suppliers so that these fees can be factored into the overall design costs.

Planning and Building Control Fees

Your local planning department will charge a set fee for a one-off dwelling when you submit your application for approval. The exact fee can be obtained from your local planning department. The Planning Fee is to cover administrative duties associated with having your application determined, but just because you have paid the fee does not guarantee that your application will be approved. Building Control Fees are set by the local Building Control Authority and are worked out on a sliding scale that is based on the estimated building cost of your house. Building Control Fees are in two parts; a Plan Fee covers the scrutiny of your application and drawings to ensure that the design conforms to the Building Regulations, and the Inspection Fee covers the construction phase of your project when your local building control officer will make periodic inspections of the works in progress.

Setting up Costs

Site Fencing

As soon as you have purchased your plot you become responsible for the safety of anyone on your land. If you are doing the building work yourself or employing sub-contractors directly, you should have the site fenced off without delay and signs put up to warn the public that it is a building site, to keep out and that appropriate safety equipment should be worn by anyone having authorized access to the site.

If you are having subcontractors work for you, you are obliged by law to provide adequate welfare facilities for them such as a toilet and a place where tea breaks can be taken with shelter from bad weather, and you are responsible for the health and safety of everyone on the site.

Insurance Costs
If you are doing the building work yourself or managing sub-contractors you will need public liability insurance once you have purchased your site and it is vital that you obtain cover and have it start immediately upon purchase. During the building process you will not only require public liability insurance but also employers' liability and contractors' all risk insurance.

Your public liability insurance covers you for people visiting your site, whether lawfully or not, or anyone outside your site, such as a neighbour, who suffers loss or injury as a result of activity on the site. Employers' liability insurance will cover you for any claim made against you by anyone that you employ to work on the site. Contractors' all risk insurance will cover you for theft of materials or tools from your site, storm, flood and fire damage and damage caused by vandalism.

Site Clearance
Depending on the nature of your site you may end up with substantial costs for site clearance and preparation to build. While the cost of excavating soil is relatively inexpensive, it can cost a considerable sum of money to have it removed from the site. Where possible, reuse all of the excavated material and have it placed. If you hit rock the cost increases dramatically and at the very least you will need to factor in the cost of a rock hammer to break up the rock.

It is important to secure your site.

Make sure you have the correct insurance cover for anyone that you employ.

Dealing with contaminated land is another potential unexpected cost that could mean the difference between a successful project and a complete disaster, so do your homework on the site properly so that you can take all of these factors into consideration. You should have a contingency sum set aside for unforeseen site conditions.

Statutory Undertaking Fees
There will be fees to pay for connecting to services including: electricity; gas; water; drainage; telephone; and roads. Once again, you should contact each of the service providers at a very early stage to get prices from them for each of the required connections and ensure that these figures are included in your budget.

Building Material Costs
You need to have an idea of how much your building materials will cost before you start building. On average material costs account for approximately one third of self-build costs. If you have been managing the whole design process properly, you should be able to generate an accurate bill of material costs and from that an accurate cost for the materials you will require. However, if you choose to buy your materials from some of the large DIY stores your costs will be much higher than if you purchase them from a specialist builder's merchant. In order to avail yourself of the lower prices you will probably have to open

an account with the merchant in order to qualify for the typical discounts offered to builders. Just as with any purchase, it is worthwhile shopping around for all the building materials you need in order to find the best deals. For this reason it is worthwhile opening accounts with a number of merchants as you will be able to compare prices. Very often one particular merchant will have very competitive prices for one or two materials and another merchant will have better prices for another material. Generally speaking, the greater the quantity of materials that you buy from one merchant, the greater the discount that will be offered. When you are seeking the best price tell the sales person the total quantity of the particular material that you are pricing so that they can give you the best possible price. Be prepared to spend time on the phone to obtain the very best prices, and do not be afraid to haggle over the prices being offered. Ask for the best discount possible, and even after you have been offered some discount, see if you can push for more. In building boom times it may be difficult to obtain competitive prices, but in times of recession, merchants will be falling over each other in order to make sales.

Merchants may be able to supply your materials VAT free but only if you have an account and they know that you are building a house for yourself. Keep a record of all your purchases, preferably in a spreadsheet, and use the running tally to ensure that you are within budget for your materials. Keep all of your receipts and invoices and file them away carefully.

Most builders' merchants will deliver materials directly to your site for little or no charge. Check on delivery charges when you are pricing and also check on availability, date and time of delivery. Remember that if you are working to a programme you will be likely to have sub-contractors organized or on site who are waiting for those materials. If the materials are not available the subcontractors will be likely to leave for another job and hold up progress on your own. Order your materials in plenty of time to avoid such hiccups. It is very useful to have a trailer or an old van to allow you to pick up materials when delivery is not available or if a merchant lets you down with a delivery; you can always pick up the materials yourself just to keep the project moving.

Bulk Materials
Sand and Aggregate
Sand and aggregate can be purchased directly from the quarry if you are prepared to buy by the lorry load. You will of course need to know how much of each material you require, but this is the most economical way of purchasing these materials. Buying from a local quarry will reduce transport-related costs. If you buy smaller quantities the cost increases dramatically, particularly if you buy these materials in bags as supplied by the DIY stores.

Cement and Concrete
If you decide to mix your own mortar or concrete on site you will need a cement mixer, but you should only do this if you are working with small quantities. Bags of cement can be purchased from most builders' merchants and your sand and aggregate as above. It is now commonplace that ready-mixed concrete is used on building sites. A mixer load of concrete contain between 4–8m³ and once again, the larger the quantity, the better the price. It may be possible to buy a half load, but check before you place the order. Concrete is expensive to get rid of and the ready-mix company will charge you more for getting rid of unused concrete than the concrete costs to make. On commercial building sites there has also been a general move away from mixing mortar on site towards purchasing ready-mixed mortar. If you are using large quantities of cement mortar and concrete then ready-mixed is the way to go.

Lime
Lime can be bought from most builders' merchants, but you should try to source local producers to reduce transport-related environmental costs. If you are using lime mortar then you will need to mix it on site. Both hydrated lime and lime putty can be mixed with sand and aggregate to produce mortar and plaster.

Bricks and Blocks and Ancillaries
Most builders' merchants will be able to supply bricks and blocks, but you will be likely to get a better deal if you go directly to the manufacturer. Some manufacturers will only supply to retailers so

Buy locally grown timber if at all possible.

check before you make your choice. Don't forget that you can use recycled bricks in your house to reduce the overall environmental footprint.

Timber and Sheet Materials
Buying locally grown timber is more sustainable than buying timber from half way round the world. If there is a sawmill close to your site, go and visit them, tell them what you are doing and see if they can supply the timber that you require. Try to purchase only timber from certified sustainable sources. Timber merchants will be able to source a wide range of timber types and sizes and will carry larger stock than most general builder's merchants and very often will offer better prices. Sheet materials such as plywood, OSB and MDF can vary considerably in price but they also vary considerably in quality. As with sawn timber, check that the timber used in the manufacture of the sheet materials is certified as

being from sustainable sources. Plasterboard and other gypsum-based boards are normally supplied by a general builder's merchant.

Plasterboard from a general builders' merchants.

113

Roofing Materials

In the recent past the roof covering for most houses was natural slate or clay roof tiles; however more recently concrete roof tiles have become popular because they have a lower capital cost. From a sustainability point of view, concrete roof tiles and fired clay tiles have more embodied energy than natural slate, but each will offer a reasonably long service life. Your local builder's merchant may only deal with a limited number of suppliers, so a search on the internet and a call to the local sales representative for the roofing material that you want may pay dividends.

'I' *section joists and laminated timber beams.*

Try to use locally sourced roofing materials.

Insulation

Given that the insulation that will be wrapped all the way around your house is the single most important contribution to reducing the lifetime environmental impact of your house, you should choose carefully. You can purchase glass fibre and mineral wool insulation at your local builder's merchants but you may need to go to specialist suppliers to obtain some of the greener insulation materials. Once again, price around but be sure that you maintain the required U-value

Specialist Timber Components

If you are using composite timber 'I' section studs or joists for the frame of your house you will more than

likely need to source these from a specialist supplier. At first glance, when you compare the cost of these components with standard solid studs they may seem expensive, but in a like-for-like situation, particularly when you want depth in the wall to accommodate increased levels of insulation, the cost makes more sense. Furthermore, when you consider that these components actually reduce the cold bridge effect associated with solid timber, then over the lifetime of the house they will pay back many times their initial cost.

Roof Trusses

If your house has cold roof construction, that is, the insulation is at ceiling level and there is a void above, then roof trusses will likely be the most economical method of forming the roof structure. There are a number of specialist manufacturers, so shop around for the best price.

Timber Frames

For standard timber frame construction, again there

are a great number of manufacturers so you should be able to get competitive quotes.

You will need to explain that the house is a very low energy house and that particular attention needs to be paid to reducing cold bridging. If the manufacturer baulks at this then be prepared to walk away. If you are building the frames yourself, then all you will require is a timber supplier, some basic tools such as a chop saw and a hammer or nail gun and you are on your way. If you are employing a joiner to build the frames once again communication is the key to achieving success. Explain the whole ethos behind the design and detailing of the house and discuss with your joiner the best way to achieve the detailing that is required to achieve low energy construction.

Windows and Doors
Unless you have a very good workshop and the skills to produce window and door profiles and to joint them, then these are best left to the specialists. There are a multitude of window and door manufacturers about so shop around for the most sustainable and cost effective components that are available.

Glass and Glazing
Low-e gas filled triple glazed units with insulating spacers should be the minimum IGU specification that you use in order to ensure that the windows are not the weak link in the building envelope. Shop around specialist glass suppliers and glazing companies to obtain the best prices. Ensure that you are being quoted like-for-like prices.

Windows and doors should generally be left to specialist manufacturers.

Drainage and Guttering

Your local builder's merchants will hold a range of uPVC drainage pipes, gutters, downpipes and fittings, but for something more sustainable you may need to pay a little more and go to a specialist supplier.

Water butts and rainwater harvesting tanks are becoming more common and you should be able to price around to get the best deal.

Plumbing Pipes and Sanitary Ware

Plumber's merchants will hold all the pipe and fitting supplies you will require. As with builder's merchants, you should open an account to benefit from the best trade discount and be ready to shop around for prices and negotiate them if required.

Drainage pipes installed at ground level.

Electrical Supplies

Your local DIY store will carry a range of wiring and fittings but for the best deals you should open an account at an electrical supplier. Wiring will be substantially cheaper as will the majority of electrical sockets and outlets. For low energy feature light fittings however, you should go to specialist suppliers.

Plastering and Tiling

Builder's merchants will be able to supply plastering materials and will often hold a limited range of tiles. Tiling should be sourced only from companies that

have good environmental credentials as the manufacture of tiles can be very energy and resource intensive. Once again shop around for the best deals.

Ironmongery

There is ironmongery and there is quality ironmongery; do not leave it to your joiner to choose or you will be disappointed. Too many houses are spoiled by the cheapest ranges of ironmongery available from the local builder's merchants. Door and window handles are but two of the few items of the fabric of your house that you actually touch on a daily basis. Go to a specialist ironmongery supplier and buy the best that you can afford. You will not regret choosing ironmongery that both feels and looks good.

Plastering complete awaiting drying out prior to second fix joinery.

Kitchens

Kitchens, like bathrooms, are very personal and you will no doubt have your own ideas about the type of kitchen that you want. If you restrict yourself to one supplier you are at their mercy with regard to price. Shop around for the best price, and do not overlook some of the large DIY sales as real bargains can be had. Shop around too for worktops and appliances as the kitchen unit supplier may not necessarily offer the best deal.

Landscaping

Because landscaping is generally the last works package on a house building programme it is often the casualty of cost overruns. Your house is not really finished until the landscaping is complete so

Kitchen tastes are personal and prices can vary significantly depending on choice.

remember to cost it fully and include it in the overall budget. There are many landscaping firms who will be happy to price your landscaping works, but if you are doing most of the work yourself, then landscaping need not break your budget. As with every other aspect of your new house, the landscaping should be properly designed to add value to your finished house. Many garden centres have designers who will prepare a planting schedule for you and will give you advice on the layout of your garden. Shop around for your plants as there are some real bargains to be had if you are prepared to buy from more than one supplier. If you go to some of the specialist growers, you may be able to negotiate good rates if you are buying in bulk.

Sub-Contractors and Labour Costs

Remember to include the cost of any additional labour or the cost of hiring sub-contractors to take on parts of the work. Ensure that they have covered everything that you expect them to cover in their tender prices, as the majority of disputes arise over misunderstandings relating to either the quality or quantity of work. Obtain all quotations in writing and ensure that the works package description that they are quoting for is properly referenced along with all of the relevant specifications and drawings. Make sure too that they zero-rate VAT on labour and any materials that they supply.

Plant Hire Costs

If you are doing the work yourself or in some instances when you are employing sub- contractors there may be specialist items of plant or equipment that you will need to hire. Check with sub-contractors when they are pricing items of work, just what equipment they will require and what equipment that they will be supplying. One cost that is often overlooked is the cost of hiring scaffolding for the duration of work on the external envelope of your house. Gone are the days of a sub-contractor hanging off the top of a ladder and overstretching to finish off the last remaining item at the top of your house, because the scaffolding has been dismantled. Programme the work so that plant and equipment that must be hired can be hired for the minimum

The Construction Process

Chapter Ten provides a step-by-step guide to the building process for both masonry and timber frame construction methods. It highlights in particular the important issues that relate to building an energy efficient building.

BEFORE YOU START ON SITE

Before you begin constructing your house you must have planning permission and, at the very least, the working drawings should be completed and have been submitted to the local building authority so that the project is registered with them. Building Control officers will want to visit the site at strategic times during the construction process to ensure that the construction is as per the drawings. It is not necessary to have Building Control permission before you start to build; however, if you choose to start on site then you need to be very confident that what you propose to build does indeed comply with the Building Regulations (see Chapter Eight for further details).

If the construction method or building materials chosen for your house are novel or unfamiliar to your local authority, which can be the case when pursuing a sustainable agenda, then you may need to prove how the construction meets the standards of the Building Regulations. In some rare cases it may be that you will only obtain Building Control approval when you have actually built the house and demonstrated beyond doubt how the construction does indeed comply with the regulations.

The project should also be registered with the Health and Safety Executive. This is to inform them that building work is about to begin and to allow them to inspect the site periodically from a health and safety perspective. If you employ a contractor then it is the contractor's responsibility to ensure that before works begin on the site that the site is a safe place to work, and that the site boundaries are secure. If you are the contractor then you have a responsibility to ensure that health and safety procedures are in place. If there is a doubt, contact relevant the health and safety authority for your area.

By this stage you should have all of your finance in place, and have agreed with the lender at what stages the monies will be released. If you are doing all the purchasing yourself, then you should also have set up accounts with builder's and plumber's merchants and other construction related suppliers in order to get the best deal on every purchase for the site.

Make sure that the site boundaries are clearly demarcated, particularly on a tight site, so that operatives that you might employ know the boundaries and work within them. Remember that your insurance will be likely to only cover work within your site, not outside it. Remember too that you should take out some form of insurance; again the type will depend on the particular building process that you have chosen. If you are the builder then you should have some form of self-build insurance in place that covers you for public and employer's liability.

Building Control should be informed that you are about to commence building operations on site and if possible tentative arrangements should be made for required inspections.

Finally, and most importantly, you should have a realistic and updated programme of works with the critical path clearly indicated. This will allow you to contact all of the sub-contractors that you plan to employ and keep them up to date with when they are expected on site. If there are slippages in the main programme that affect any of the sub-contractors then you will be in a position to inform them of the delay.

Your Programme of Work is a very important document. You should try where possible to group work packages together where the plant and machinery that is required is the same, or where deliveries from a particular supplier can be grouped so as to cut down carbon emissions from operations on site.

It is worth contacting all of the immediate neighbours around the site to inform them of works starting on site and letting them know when you expect completion.

TASKS COMMON TO TIMBER AND MASONRY CONSTRUCTION

Whether you are building a timber-framed house or a masonry house, the first few steps of construction are the same, as are the last few. The main difference is in the above-ground, load-bearing superstructure. Setting up actions, measuring and accurately setting out the foundations, earthworks, and drainage actions are all common to masonry and timber construction at the start of the building process. At the end of the process, second fix joinery, second fix mechanical, and electrical, commissioning, finishes and site-works and landscaping are also common to both methods of construction.

STARTING ON SITE

Setting-up (Common to both Timber and Masonry Construction)

A building site can be a very busy place. Space should be allocated to carry out all of the necessary work activities in a safe manner and space should also be

---

Before You Begin Building Checklist

- Do you have planning permission to build your house? (*See* Chapter Four for details.)
- Do you know where the exact site boundaries are? (*See* Chapter Five for details.)
- Have you secured the site boundary to HSE standards? (*See* this chapter for details.)
- Are the working/construction drawings complete? (*See* Chapter Eight for details.)
- Have you a detailed written programme of building work for each stage of the build process? (*See* Chapter Two for details.)
- Do you have finance in place for the construction phase? (*See* Chapter Nine for details.)
- Have you agreed with the lender at what stages the monies will be released? (*See* Chapter Nine for details.)
- Have you set up accounts with local Builder's Merchants and other suppliers? (*See* Chapter Nine for details.)
- Have you checked to ensure that they can supply timber from sustainable sources? (*See* Chapter Seven for details.)
- Have you submitted an application to Building Control? (*See* Chapter Eight for details.)
- Have you informed Building Control that you are about to start operations on site? (*See* Chapter Eight for details.)
- Do you have the necessary insurances in place for the particular build process? (*See* Chapter Two for details.)
- Have you contacted all of your sub-contractors to inform them that building works are about to begin? (*See* Chapter Two for details.)
- Have you informed the neighbours around the site that works are about to commence and given them an idea of when works should be complete?

allocated to the storage of construction materials and waste. Check all of the drawings including the drainage and service installation drawings to enable these to be marked on the site. What you are trying to avoid here is double handling of materials or having to move some item in order to carry out an element of work. It is important to make every job count. Furthermore, if you are employing tradesmen to work on your house then you will need to set space aside for welfare facilities. Make sure your statutory health and safety information is on display in a visible location at the site entrance and that other health and safety information is placed on a notice board. None of the above should be left to chance, but instead should be carefully planned to maximize efficiency on the site from day one. One additional very important item; make sure that all of the existing services on or immediately adjacent to the site are located and clearly marked to avoid inadvertently hitting them. In addition, make sure that all operatives allowed on site are inducted into safety procedures and that they are made aware of all potential site hazards. It is vital that you secure the site at this stage if you have not already done so.

Setting-out (Common to Both Timber and Masonry Construction)

All construction work begins with setting out the location of the building on the site normally using points on, around or within the established site boundaries. Setting-out must be carried out in both the horizontal and vertical planes.

Horizontal setting-out is particularly important on tight sites where there is just sufficient room for your house to fit, as you do not want to build on someone else's property. Furthermore, the exact location of your house will be shown on the approved planning drawings and should not deviate from this position. It is not uncommon for house builders to have to demolish or partially demolish buildings that do not comply with the planning drawings. Vertical setting-out establishes the relationship between floor levels and the existing ground level. This again is important from a planning perspective, and vertical setting out also has an implication in relation to disabled access and to such things as drainage connections. It is good practice to have a setting-out drawing prepared by your designer that will allow you to position the house in accordance with the planning drawings. Setting-out is always carried out with reference to some features on the site or site boundary that are unlikely to change during the construction process. There is little point in taking dimensions from some structure that is going to be demolished or removed as soon as building operations begin. Where possible, the setting-out of the house should coincide with the longest dimension on your house plan and can be

Mark out the site from the boundary and define the building area using profile boards (photograph © Mark Forkin, NuTech Renewables Ltd.).

Profile boards are used to keep the building footprint square and provide known levels (photograph © Mark Forkin, NuTech Renewables Ltd.).

either the width or depth of the house. If you do this there is less chance of the actual position of your house deviating from the position on the drawings.

Exact points can be fixed using triangulation from other fixed objects or points and pegs can be driven into the ground at these points. Always check to ensure that the setting-out lines are square.

Corner profile boards are used to set out straight lines and are kept out of the way of the excavations. They can also be used to establish a level providing their level is known.

Earthworks, Drainage, Public Utilities and Inspections (Common to both Timber and Masonry Construction)

All of the topsoil must be removed from the whole of the footprint area of the house. The reason for doing this is that it contains organic matter, which if left under the house, through time would rot causing differential settlement of the ground and possibly the house too. Before you remove the topsoil however, check for wild grass and wild flower content and where there is potentially valuable biodiversity, carefully set the turf aside and ensure it re-establishes in its new location. Removed topsoil should either be spread on the garden or, if space on site is tight, it should be set aside in a spoil heap that is out of the way of any building operations, but in all cases, try to limit the size of spoil heaps. Topsoil should be used to create garden areas on the site when building operations are complete or, if space does not permit a garden, then it should be sold off or given away locally. It is worth setting up composting areas on site for the duration of the construction phase. You should rake all grass and leaves off the excavation area and mulch all branches and twigs and compost in their own area. Topsoil can be added to the composting areas and when the construction phase is finished you should have a good supply of rich deep compost that can be used to enrich existing topsoil for garden areas.

If there is hard standing on site in the way of your excavations, carefully grub it up and, where possible reuse it as hardcore. Also, if other more valuable materials have been used such as stone sets, then they can be recycled and used to construct new areas of paved landscaping.

The location of foundations should be marked and excavated to the required levels. Building control should be notified to allow them to inspect the excavations to check that the ground conditions are adequate to bear the intended loads. Any drainage lines should be marked and excavated if appropriate.

123

Try to avoid taking any topsoil or subsoil away from the site. At the site investigation stage you may have identified that a partially buried building be appropriate on your site. In this instance, the soil should be set aside until the retaining building fabric has been constructed and then carefully placed against and over the building structure to create a buffer layer of insulating earthwork.

Where ground conditions are poor and there is a requirement for piling, there is further opportunity to use renewable or recycled materials in a way that is not as permanent or damaging than conventional piling. Timber piles are used in many countries and have the great advantage of being a renewable resource. Care must be taken in the choice of timber used to ensure that it is from a sustainable source and that it is rot resistant. Where soil conditions allow, recycled aggregate can be used for piles by using dynamic vibration and compaction. If concrete piles are required, then consider piles that are made with recycled aggregate and have at least some cement substitution. Sheet steel piles can be used instead of concrete retaining walls and have the ability to be removed and recycled at the end of the building's life.

When using mechanical excavation equipment there should always be a banks-man present whose job it is to work closely with the operator and to be their eyes and ears. It is virtually impossible for the operator of an excavator to see what it is that they are digging up especially when the excavator's arm is fully extended. The presence of a banks-man is particularly important when working in the vicinity of existing services. All excavations around services should be carried out by hand, regardless of how skilful the plant operator is. Striking a buried electricity cable can be fatal for the operator or even the banks-man, and striking other buried services can be costly in financial terms and also in time. Remember too that deep excavations are particularly dangerous and that ground around such excavations can collapse suddenly and without warning. If in doubt, consult with your local health and safety body with regard to safe methods of working in such instances.

If you have a sloping site that requires retaining of terraces it is worth considering using gabions filled with clean stone or rubble material cleared from the site. Gabions filled with uniform material are attrac-tive in their own right, and those filled with a variety of materials can be over-planted to create a living retaining wall feature. It is also possible to create reinforced earth-retaining walls using good quality subsoil from the site. Lime can be used to stabilize soil to provide a base for floor slabs or hard standing. The advantage of using lime is that the process can be undone at the end of the life of the structure.

Foundations, Sub-floor and Inspections (Common to both Timber and Masonry Construction)

Foundation Concrete

Foundation concrete is used to spread the load of the walls of the house across a larger surface area. Most concrete used for foundations is of the ready-mixed type that is batch-mixed to known strengths and delivered to site using cement-mixer lorries. Ensure that receipts and delivery dockets are kept on file in case of problems further down the line. A rule-of-thumb for the width of foundation required is calculated by taking the width of the wall to be constructed and adding to each side of the wall the depth of the concrete required. Thus, if your engineer has requested foundations that are 250mm deep, and if your wall thickness is 350mm, then the foundations will be 250mm + 350mm + 250mm = 850mm total width. Excavations for foundations should be notified to the building control inspector to allow for inspection prior to pouring of the concrete.

Damp Proof Membranes

Due to the presence of groundwater, and the uncanny ability of this water to find its way through floor constructions and reveal itself as rising damp, a damp proof membrane (DPM) is normally required across the full sub-floor preparations. The most common material that is used for damp proof membranes is polythene sheet.

Drains Before they are Covered up

Any drainage that is required to run under the building is obviously required to be in place before the ground floor is constructed. It is important that drainage locations are marked accurately and the up-

Polythene damp proof membrane laid prior to insulating the floor slab.

stands placed in exactly the right locations before any floor concrete is poured in particular. Once trenches have been excavated and the drainage pipes bedded in pea-gravel, Building Control should be informed so that they can carry out inspections before the drainage is back filled.

Remember that foul and rainwater (storm) drainage should be kept separate where possible. Even if there are combined foul and storm drains, if you can do away with the requirement to discharge

Drainage pipes laid in pea gravel.

your rainwater by installing a rainwater harvesting system, then you should do so. Often, storm drainage is installed after the house is constructed when the contractor is tidying up the site, prior to completing the landscaping. This prevents rainwater gullies and underground pipes being damaged during the construction process.

Drains After they are Covered up (Backfilled and Ready for Testing)
Once the drains have been backfilled it is normal practice to pressure test the drainage installation to ensure that there are no leaks before the pipes become inaccessible under the floor.

The Ground Floor and Inspections (Common to both Timber and Masonry Construction)

There are two principal ways of constructing the ground floor for a timber frame building. A concrete floor will be constructed directly on top of the sub-floor preparations, whereas a suspended timber or concrete floor requires a ventilation space between the sub-floor and the floor structure itself. In each case the perimeter walls should be built up from the foundations to the required level. The height to which the walls are built depends on the detail that is to be used at this location. In both situations the one detail that is critical to low energy construction is achieving continuity of insulation between the floor and the external walls. This will be discussed in detail later. The further detail, which is critical to build-ability of the timber frame, is that the perimeter wall (or edge of slab) that the timber frame will bear on should be as level as possible with no more than plus or minus 5mm corner to corner run-off.

Concrete Floor on Grade
The first layer in a concrete floor on grade is normally hard fill or hardcore. If there have been demolitions on the site or local to the site then some of the demolition materials may be suitable for reuse as hardcore, otherwise crushed stone is normally used. Hardcore should be laid in layers not exceeding 150mm and should be well rammed and compacted between each layer. It is normal practice to lay some

Sand blinding levelled prior to laying DPC (photograph © Mark Forkin, NuTech Renewables Ltd.).

form of fine blinding material on top of the hardcore.

The material used is normally quarry dust or sand and can have a variety of functions depending on what is laid directly on top of it. If a concrete (structural) sub-floor is to be laid directly on top of the hardcore, the fine blinding material helps to prevent the fines in the concrete from disappearing through the sometimes large gaps in the hardcore. If the next layer to be laid over the blinding is the damp proof membrane (DPM) then the blinding helps prevent sharp stones in the hardcore from puncturing the membrane. If the insulation is to be laid directly over the blinding then it provides a level surface for the insulation to be laid on. (On a purely practical note, it is more difficult to get the hardcore level than sand or quarry dust.) Normally the damp proof membrane is laid at this point, and if there is to be a structural concrete sub-floor then the concrete will be poured directly on top of the damp proof membrane. After this the walls will be constructed and only then will the insulation be laid on top of the concrete sub-floor before pouring the screed. Services can be laid over or

under the insulation and a sand/cement or concrete finishing screed is then laid on top of the insulation when finishes are under way. The major drawback with laying screeds at the finishing off stage however, is that there is so much moisture introduced into what should be a very dry house built from very dry timber, that it simply does not make sense.

An alternative layering of the floor, which uses less concrete, is to place the insulation on top of the damp-proof membrane and then to pour the concrete slab directly on top of the insulation. The concrete is then levelled off by power floating to such a degree that it is level enough to receive floor finishes if any additional finishes are to be used. The major advantage of using this type of floor is that there is no requirement for a finishing screed at a later stage in the construction process and this therefore reduces the quantity of construction moisture that is introduced to what should be a very dry building. The one major disadvantage is that services are more difficult to include within the floor slab as the slab is the finished floor, and as yet no walls have been constructed. If

Rigid board insulation laid prior to pouring concrete.

they are to be included within the floor the pipe and duct runs for cables have to be buried under the slab and need to surface in the exact locations using this method of floor construction.

Suspended Concrete Floor

A suspended concrete floor uses pre-cast concrete slabs or beams (with infill) that are supported at the ends by the perimeter walls and span between these and any intermediate supporting walls. One advantage of using a suspended concrete floor is that it can speed up the construction process somewhat in that the floor can be laid quickly and because there is no curing required it is immediately available for building on. The build-up on top of the suspended slab is then much the same as for a concrete, on grade-type floor. One disadvantage of using pre-cast concrete slabs is that a crane or other type of mechanical plant is required to lift the slabs into place. Concrete beams with infill blocks on the other hand can in some instances be lifted into place by hand and the infill blocks are capable of being positioned by hand. Traditionally concrete was used to make the infill blocks but there are also clay infill blocks on the market that would be more environmentally friendly than concrete. There are also beam and infill products on the market that utilize insulation infill blocks but be sure to use only systems that have insulation under or around

the beams because, without this insulation, each beam becomes a cold bridge where heat can escape.

Suspended Timber Floor

Suspended timber floors are built off a timber base-plate that rests on a damp proof course (DPC) that is laid on the foundation walls. If packing is required under the baseplate to make it level, ensure that the packing is solid and not just under individual floor joists. As well as giving a level surface to build off, the baseplate helps spread the load from individual joists along the length of the foundation wall. Solid bridging or rim-joists should be used directly under where load-bearing walls will rest on the floor.

Regardless of the type of floor construction used in a timber-frame house, it is vital that the foundation wall or floor is both square and level directly under where the external walls are located. If not, the walls will run out of true and it will be virtually impossible to get the roof level and square with resulting difficulties in aligning slates and tiles particularly along the roof verge.

MASONRY CONSTRUCTION

Setting-out – Critical Dimensions

Masonry walls are usually built using two skins (or leaves or writhes) that are tied together across a cavity using wall ties. The purpose of the cavity is twofold. The first purpose is to create a water barrier to prevent water penetrating to the inner skin, and the second is to form an insulating layer of relatively still air. It is a widely held misconception that brickwork is waterproof. In the majority of cases, bricks are themselves porous, meaning that they will absorb moisture from the rain that will find its way to the inner surface, particularly under driving rain conditions. Furthermore, the cement mortar that is normally used to keep the bricks apart always shrinks during and after the curing process. The result of this shrinking is that there are numerous hair cracks that form between the mortar and the bricks that create a ready-made water path for driving rain to penetrate to the inside of the cavity.

If using facing brick as the outer skin, then the outer brickwork skin is the critical dimension for setting-out. The reason for this is to ensure that the

Setting-out is important and if carried out properly will save time and effort later (photograph © Keith Lockhart).

wall lengths and opening sizes are coordinated with standard brickwork dimensions so that there are no unsightly cut bricks or stretched joints externally where they will be seen. The setting-out for block-work that will be covered with render or plaster is much less critical and, like timber frame construc-tion, the inner skin may be used for setting out. In masonry cavity wall construction as in timber frame construction it is the inner skin only that is the load-bearing element.

The Ground Floor (Possible Joinery First Fix)

Ground floors can be of almost any construction type such as solid concrete on grade, suspended concrete or suspended timber as per timber frame construc-tion. Floor topping similarly can be almost any common material such as sand/cement, concrete, or floating timber. If the floors are to be suspended timber or suspended concrete then ventilation bricks should be built in to the sub-floor walls to provide sufficient under-floor airflow to comply with the relevant building regulation.

The Walls and Openings

Masonry walls are traditionally built brick on brick, block on block using sand cement mortar. (There are some prefabricated methods of block construction using lightweight, aerated concrete blocks, factory bonded together to form panels, but these methods have not yet been widely adopted in the construction industry.) Ground floor openings are formed as the walls are built upwards. If a standard cavity wall is being created it is vital that the cavity is kept clear of mortar droppings, particularly at wall ties. Mortar that bridges the cavity forms a path for water to pass across the cavity from the outer leaf to the inner leaf.

TIMBER FRAME CONSTRUCTION

The Frame, Walls and Openings (Timber Frame)

With any timber frame construction it is vital that the frame is erected as quickly as possible and kept as dry as possible. There is little point in using well dried out timber if it is allowed to become wet on site.

It is generally considered good practice to have the timber frame wall components constructed off site in factory conditions and only delivered to site when required. This will ensure that the materials remain dry, and in most instances that there is a high degree of quality control. If however the wall frames are to be manufactured on site then it is good practice to manufacture these under cover, store them under cover and then erect them as above making sure that the wood remains as dry as possible throughout. If however, the wall frames are exposed for any length of time to the rain and become soaked, the building should be made weather-tight and before the insulation and dry-lining are installed, the timber should be allowed to dry out to a moisture content of around sixteen per cent as this will be around the equilibrium moisture content. If however, the framing timber is to dry at around eight to ten per cent then it is good practice once again to let the timber reach its equilibrium of around sixteen per cent otherwise the timber will have a tendency to split when being nailed.

Traditional timber frame construction

In traditional mass produced timber frame construction the frames are normally delivered to the site with the sheathing ply already fixed to the frame and the building wrap already fixed to the external face of the ply. It is normal practice for frames to be manufactured from kiln-dried timber. If the frames are erected immediately on delivery to the site then the house can be made weather tight in a short space of time and all of the timber used in the house kept dry. If however the frames are going to be sitting around on site for any period of time, then they should be stored horizontally or vertically as per the instructions from the manufacturer and fully protected from the weather. In the past it was considered adequate simply to staple the overlaps of the building wrap. Today however, due to the ever-increasing requirements for air tightness, all the overlaps should be taped at all vertical and horizontal junctions to form an airtight barrier. It is also important to ensure that all openings in or penetrations of the building wrap be taped as well. In some instances around openings, and around flashings in particular, additional skirts of

Timber frames should be protected from the weather where possible (photograph © Keith Lockhart).

Non standard frames are fixed in much the same way as standard timber frames (photograph © Keith Lockhart).

building wrap will need to be taped on to ensure that water that finds its way through the building envelope is directed back to the outside.

Alternative Timber Frame Construction
With non-traditional timber frame construction the construction process is much the same as with traditional frame construction. The main differences lie in the materials that are used and the amount of prefabrication that may take place prior to erection.

Materials
There are now a great many engineered timber products on the market that are suitable replacements for solid timber framing members. A number of these take the form of 'I' section timbers that have soft-wood or plywood or LVL flanges with a plywood or oriented strand board (OSB) or hardboard web.

The reasons for manufacturing such products include the reduction in the overall quantity of timber used, the ability to achieve consistent high strength and the ability to produce uniform high-grade products out of low-grade timber. From a sustainability point of view the reduction in timber use has an overall beneficial effect in preserving timber resources and thus preserving sequestrated carbon. The greater depth that can be achieved with ease using such products means that greater depths of insulation can be used between the framing members making them particularly suitable for energy efficient construction. Furthermore, the narrow section of the web means that there is less heat-loss through the framing member compared to a solid framing member of the same depth or strength. There are a number of other benefits including workability and handle-ability that can be beneficial in the construction process. Furthermore, because of the inherent strength associated with some of the deeper sizes of engineered timber studs the requirement for noggins is reduced and in some instances they may not be required at all. The benefit of having no noggins is that the insulation layer is more continuous, and there is a reduction in labour cost.

Prefabrication

The more prefabrication the faster will be the construction on site and if carried out in factory conditions quality control should be greater. The amount of prefabrication will very much depend on the detailed design of the walls, roof and floor elements. To a certain degree, traditional timber frame manufacturing already has a certain level of prefabrication, but this only extends to the framing members, the external sheathing and the building wrap. Access is required to the spaces between the framing members to fit wiring and plumbing and any other building services that may be required and all before the insulation is fitted in the same voids. With the drive towards more airtight construction, the building wrap may not be sufficient to create the airtight barrier required so a second line of defence is called for. This can take the form of an air barrier placed to the inner side of the studs. If this is factory fitted then there is no longer access on site to the cavities between the framing members so the insulation also has to be factory fitted before the air barrier. The prefabricated frames can then be delivered to site and erected and the air barrier kept intact. Battens are factory or site fixed to the inner face of the external walls and a service void created to allow services to be installed on site. There is obviously a weight penalty with additional prefabrication and the use of a crane is required on site to erect the heavier panels. In a similar way, floor and roof panels (cassettes) can be prefabricated and erected at the relevant stage in the process.

Intermediate Floors (Inspections)

If the house is two storeys or more, the intermediate

LVL and OSB engineered timber members (photograph © Keith Lockhart).

floors are normally laid as soon as the ground floor walls are in place. The floor then forms a platform from which the upper floor wall panels can be erected and hence the name, 'platform construction'. If the floor boards are laid at the same time as the floor joists, then it is imperative that the building be erected in as short a space of time as possible to keep the floors dry.

This will ensure that the joints between the boards remain tight. Building control should be informed when intermediate floors are in place to allow for inspection. Once again you should consider using

Timber floors should be kept dry to prevent warping.

131

engineered timber products for floor joist members. Some engineered floor joists, such as those with a metal lattice web, will allow services to be installed relatively easily, including ducts for whole house heat recovery mechanical ventilation.

Air-tightness (Common to both Timber and Masonry Construction)

One of the most critical areas in a well-insulated low energy building is the air barrier. The location of the air barrier should have been considered carefully at the design stage and should be given special attention during the construction stage.

OSB with the joints taped contributing to airtightness in this timber frame house.

Installation of the air barrier is a vital part in constructing an energy-efficient home.

If you are not physically doing the work yourself then it is wise either to take on the role or appoint someone in the role of 'air barrier manager'. Each member of the project team should be reminded of the importance of the air barrier, and the air barrier should be specifically mentioned in contract documentation and information given to subcontractors. The air barrier should be inspected regularly and particular attention should be given to it before it is closed in and becomes inaccessible. When the building is at the wind and water tight stage an air-tightness test should be carried out by a specialist. If there are leaks in the air barrier this will show up in the air-tightness testing. It is preferable not to close in any of the air barrier until the air tightness

is complete as leaks in the air barrier can easily be remedied if the air barrier is readily accessible. The results of the air tightness testing should be forwarded to your local building control as required. It is important to seal each and every joint in the air barrier using proprietary tape designed for the purpose.

Do not be tempted to take shortcuts, and do not attempt to use some other type of tape, otherwise you run the risk of the tape joint failing within a few years and the house leaking air like a sieve.

Inform Building Control when roof timbers are in place (photograph © Keith Lockhart).

Closing in the building and getting the roof on quickly are vital in timber frame construction (photograph © Keith Lockhart).

The Roof and Inspections (common to both timber and masonry construction)

Once again, when it comes to the roof, it is important to erect it as quickly as possible in order to make the house wind and water tight as quickly as possible.

If prefabricated trusses are being used these should be stored as per the manufacturer's recommendations and once again the moisture content of the timber (the bottom chord in particular) should be at around sixteen per cent before being sheeted with the lining material. If using roof timbers cut on site the same principle applies; the ceiling joists should be allowed to reach their equilibrium moisture content before being dry lined. Building control should be informed when the roof timbers are in place to allow for inspection.

Wind and Water tight (Common to both Timber and Masonry Construction)

Regardless of the type of construction, it is always an achievement when the building is considered wind and water tight. In many instances it is one of the payment stages where banks will release funds against an architect's certificate. The wind and water tight stage is reached when the walls, windows and doors, roof and roof covering are in place and all of the potential air paths sealed.

Get the windows and doors installed early to help achieve a weathertight enclosure.

Where possible, this is when the air pressure test should be carried out as it allows any air leakage paths to be quickly identified and remedied. This of course assumes that there will be no further penetrations in the air barrier and that all services will be kept to the inside of the barrier. It is always good practice to keep all services to the inside so that there are no unexpected air leakage paths. If the inner lining boards are

One of the difficulties in placing the air barrier next to the plasterboard is that it is penetrated by all the services.

part of the air barrier, then all gaps around sockets and pipes and all conduits that may provide continuity of air leakage paths should be sealed before carrying out the air pressure test.

When the building is wind and water tight, this marks the stage when items that are susceptible to damage from the weather can be installed internally. The achievement of the weather-tight stage means that further delays caused by inclement weather will be limited to external works only and the interior can be finished off in dry conditions.

Building Services First and Second Fix (Common to both Timber and Masonry Construction)

The first fix of building services includes the fixing of conduits and back boxes for electrical works, and all concealed pipe runs and ducts for mechanical works. The building services, like every other aspect of the construction of your house must be coordinated both in design and construction.

Plumbing and wiring below a linen cupboard.

At the design stage, thought should have been given to the location of every building service component with a view to minimizing the length of service runs and sufficient space should have been allocated to incorporate everything required. This is particularly important when a whole house ventilation system is to be installed. A ventilation system requires reasonably large service voids to ensure adequate room for the ductwork to be installed. In addition, when obtaining prices for works packages such as wiring and plumbing, you should spell out clearly that you are building a sustainable house, and that elements such as the air barrier must be left intact when installing their particular works package. You should also state that an allowance should be made in their price for coordinating their work with that of other trades and works packages. This way there is no excuse for claims for extras when consideration has to be given to routing one particular service element around another. Furthermore, before allowing any electrical or mechanical trades loose on your house to install their particular works package, you should at the very least hold a meeting with all of them together to coordinate the total services installation. The more communication there is between each of the trades working on your house, the greater will be the coordination of every element and the better will be the final product. At this meeting it should be stressed what it is that you are trying to achieve and explain about the importance of the integrity of the air barrier. In most house building, the electricians and plumbers would normally make the decisions as to where their service runs should be located. This will normally involve routing the services around the house in the shortest most practical way and usually involves drilling through floor

and ceiling joists and studs in traditional wall frames. In masonry construction vertical chases in walls should not be deeper than one-third of the wall thickness or in cavity walls one-third of the thickness of the leaf.

Horizontal chases should not be deeper than one-sixth of the thickness of the leaf or wall. Chases should not be so positioned as to impair the stability of the wall. This is particularly important where hollow blocks are used.

When building an energy-efficient house however, the services will probably be located in a specially created service void to the inside of the air barrier. From a quality control point of view, check that holes are drilled in the correct location, and that where floor joists have been notched, that the notches are not too deep so as to weaken the timber. Regardless of whether the house is of masonry or timber frame

Concrete walls need to be chased to install first fix wiring.

Socket and switch heights should conform to building control requirements.

construction, the requirements for notches and holes in supportive floor and roof joists is given in the IEE regulations 1B 6 of Section A1. Any notches in timber studs or joists with services behind should not be so deep that they affect the structural integrity of the framing member and the wiring should be contained within an earthed metal conduit to prevent someone from inadvertently driving a nail through the pipe or wire. Building control should be notified at the stage of 'first fix' or 'pre-plaster', before electrical wiring, structural elements such as lintels and beams and insulation materials concealed in walls, floors or roof spaces are covered by render, plaster or plasterboard. Remember that socket outlets and switches should be located at heights to comply with the relevant Building Regulation that deals with access for the disabled. In most instances this will mean that sockets and switches should be located within a zone 450mm above floor level to 1200mm above floor level. Any additional wiring for automatic fire detection and alarm systems or smoke alarm systems should also be installed at first-fix stage.

Included within your first-fix installations will be socket outlets, lighting, telephone outlets, communications sockets, television and satellite and if you are including any other built-in appliances that require power such as a central vacuum system then a power supply will be required adjacent to the proposed installation point.

Heating and Ventilation

Where a whole house ventilation system is to be installed, ideally this should be done before any other service and the other service runs routed around the installed ductwork. If for some reason it is not installed first, then make sure that the trades installing the other services are made aware of the routes for the ductwork and of the requirement to leave adequate space for the ductwork.

Electrical

Ducts with draw cords inserted are laid from the electricity source to the entry point to the electricity meter cupboard. The incoming electricity cable is installed by the electricity service provider within the ducts laid by you or your contractor.

Connection Fees and Temporary Supply

There are connection fees that must be paid to the relevant statutory service providers. It is worth checking with the local office for each to ensure that the lead-in times are not too long. If they are lengthy, then obviously you should place your order in plenty of time. It is sometimes worthwhile arranging to have a temporary supply of electricity installed to assist with the construction of your house. This will require full certification by an electrician before it can be used, but if you locate it in a position where it can be incorporated into the wall of the house or garage, then it can remain in place after the house is built and it will save having to move it.

The Electricity Meter

Electricity meters should be located within a weather-tight enclosure where they can be read by the electricity company without having to gain access to your house. These are often located on an external house wall, but could equally be located in a garage

Wiring loom for consumer unit placed in a central location to reduce wiring runs.

wall or shed wall providing it complies with the current IEE regulation.

The Consumer Unit

The location of the distribution board will dictate the origin of all of the wiring runs. It goes without saying that the more centrally located the distribution board is then the shorter will be the cable runs. This should save a little on material and installation costs.

Wiring

Wiring should be installed by a competent person to the latest edition of the Institute of Electrical Engineers (IEE) Regulations and care should be taken to ensure that where cables are installed where they are laid against or surrounded by insulation that they are up-rated sufficiently (this is to prevent the wires from overheating and causing a fire). Also note that there are some insulation materials that can attack the PVC insulation on the wires, so always be careful when wiring is installed in close proximity to insulation materials.

Earth Bonding

Any exposed metalwork such as a sink or radiator should be connected to the earth terminal of the electrical wiring system to prevent them carrying live current as a result of a fault in the wiring system. This is known as earth bonding. Incoming water and gas pipes should be earth bonded as they enter the house, any exposed structural steel and metal in bathrooms should also be earth bonded and all services must be interconnected by earth bonding.

Cables in Walls

Cables that are buried in walls should run either vertically or horizontally so that their path can be easily traced once they have been covered in.

Hot and Cold Water

There should be a stop valve (stop cock)/isolating valve at the boundary of the property and in certain areas of the country a water meter will be installed in this location as well. The incoming cold water supply (normally referred to as the rising main) should be insulated where it comes through the ground floor to prevent condensation on the cold pipe. There should

be an isolating valve located in a convenient location where the rising main enters the house and if a pressure reducing valve is required in the system then this is an ideal location for this too. The route that the rising water main then takes is very dependent on the type of hot and cold water systems that are to be installed in the house.

Hot water cylinder location with pipe tails installed.

Joinery Second Fix (Floor/Wall and Ceiling linings) (Common to both Timber and Masonry Construction)

Having installed all of the services and all of the insulation within the wall and ceiling cavities, the wall and ceiling linings can now be installed. The Building Regulations require precautions to be taken to inhibit the spread of fire within a building. The requirements for the internal linings are that they should adequately resist the spread of flame over their surfaces and, if ignited, have a rate of heat release that is reasonable in the circumstances. Most gypsum-based boards have these properties inherently, and are thus used for wall and ceiling linings. Before installing any wallboards however, you should ensure that there are adequate 'grounds' (additional timber framing or plywood fixed between the framing members) for fixing items to. This is particularly important if your house is to be lined with plasterboard, as there are many fixtures and fittings that are just too heavy for plasterboard to support. Even though you will have considered fixtures and fittings at the design stage, it is well worth walking around the house before any linings are in place and asking yourself the question for every wall in the house, what is going to be on this wall? Mark up on a drawing where additional grounds are required and make sure these are in place before the linings are fitted. Cellulose-reinforced gypsum boards tend to be denser and have greater load-bearing capacity and pull-out strength than standard plasterboard and may therefore not require the same extent of additional grounds. It is better to be safe than sorry so if you are in doubt as to what exactly you are going to fit or if you have not yet decided where exactly you are going to fit things then you would be better off with the denser board that will cut down the amount of grounds required.

Dry Lining Finishing (Common to both Timber and Masonry Construction)

When the dry lining is completed the joints between boards and nail holes in the boards should be filled and sanded before other trades complete their second fix. This allows the dry liners to work on uncluttered surfaces and should ensure a high quality of finish. Dry lining is not a dry process as the name suggests, but it is certainly much drier than traditional plastering. Plastering is considered a wet trade and during the plastering process large quantities of moisture are introduced to what is otherwise a dry building. With dry lining the quantity of water involved is negligible, and thus it is more suitable when trying to maintain an even level of moisture content within the construction. This will help ensure that the timber frame does not move through fluctuating moisture content. With dry lining only the joints and nail holes are filled with a fine plaster-like substance called jointing compound. The rest of the board surface is the finished surface. To fill the joints a little jointing compound is applied the full length of the joint and a reinforcing tape is pushed into the wet compound and immediately a further slightly wider application of jointing compound is applied on top of the reinforcing tape and the edges finished level with the edge of the taper on the board edge. As the jointing compound dries it shrinks back

a little and creates a slight hollow. When this layer has set, a further wider still layer of jointing/finishing compound is applied and this time the edges of the new jointing compound are extended out over the tapered edges of the board. The edges of this last layer are feathered into the board surface so that the appearance is of a solid surface with no joints in the board. Ideally there should be minimal sanding of the jointing compound surfaces as this tends to raise some of the fibres on the board surface, but where it is necessary it should be blended in with the rest of the board to ensure that paint finishes do not appear to be patchy.

Plaster Finishing (Common to both Timber and Masonry Construction)

If you are using solid plaster or plasterboard and skim finish instead of dry lining then, just as with dry lining finishing, once the first fix electrical and plumbing is finished and any stud walls and ceilings have been boarded then it is time to plaster.

Each layer of plaster requires a good key and the correct plasters should be used for each location. On plasterboard a bonding coat should be applied then a skim coat. Cement-based plasters such as are common in Ireland are prone to cracking as the cement component shrinks as it dries just as with any other cement-based product. Try to avoid using cement-based plasters where possible.

Building Services Second Fix (Common to both Timber and Masonry Construction)

Second fix electrical and plumbing is when sockets, switches, sinks, wash-hand basins and such like are fitted. Before fitting such items it is important to ensure that the surfaces that they are being fixed to are indeed finished (except for paint) and do not require any additional work. It can become expensive if you have to get tradesmen back to remove items and then have to replace them. Each fitting should be fully tested and commissioning certificates should be obtained from the electrician and plumber for each element they have fitted and tested.

When designing the layout of your electrical systems, do not forget to include a burglar alarm.

Try to avoid using cement-based plasters where possible.

This item will give you peace of mind and very often will reduce your house insurance premiums. Many people have an aversion to electrical items that are complicated to use. When choosing your system, ensure that the controls are easy to use by all, that way you will actually use them. Better to install a simple system that is actually used than an all singing all dancing complicated system that is never used. Regardless of the actual alarm system used, there are two main detectors used universally. These are the magnetic break contact detectors such as are attached to windows and doors that set the alarm off when the door or window is opened, and the infrared detector that detects the heat given off by a body moving in the path of the detector. Infrared detectors are often located at the corners of rooms at ceiling height. Other types of sensors include pressure plates and beam sensors that can be used strategically to

improve the overall security of your house and garden. Many people do not alarm the upper floors of their houses, thinking that burglars only break in at ground floor level. Burglars are wise to this and often break in at first floor level, ransack the first floor and leave by the same way they entered. It is therefore worth alarming your whole house and creating separate zones that can be isolated when in use.

Outside your house you may wish to use movement sensors or beam detectors to operate low energy security lighting. Try where possible to minimize false alarms caused by animals setting off the lights.

Finishing Joinery (Common to both Timber and Masonry Construction)

Finishing joinery as the name suggests is the stage when finished joinery items are fitted. Doors are hung and ironmongery attached, architraves and skirting are fitted, stairs are finished off with balustrades and handrails, kitchen units are fitted, and any other items of finishing joinery are installed.

Finishes (Common to both Timber and Masonry Construction)

For high quality finishes there are three things to remember: preparation, preparation and preparation. Surfaces should be sanded smooth where required,

Ensure plaster is sufficiently dry before applying finishes.

The external envelope is more critical than the internal finishes.

to be completed. If you have to bring back trades there will be delays and often things will be overlooked because they are simply put into the 'too hard' box.

Internal

Just as with the external envelope, the interior should be finished off in a systematic manner. Try to finish off discrete work packages and ensure that the quality of workmanship does not deteriorate just to get the work finished on time. Again it is a useful exercise to take the house room by room and create a list of outstanding items. Be systematic with how you approach each room; for example, start with the ceiling, then the door wall then move from left to right, top to bottom for each wall and finish with the floor. This way you should be able to list everything that is outstanding and allow you to finish everything off in a systematic manner.

Commissioning of Services
Before you use any of the mechanical or electrical

Be systematic in finishing off each room.

142

Finish off discrete work elements so that you do not have to re-erect scaffolding.

services in the house make sure these have been systematically commissioned by the relevant trade and signed off as safe, fully operational and complying with the relevant regulations. Furthermore, ensure that you have the relevant manuals for each piece of equipment and ensure that you are completely conversant with their operation before use. Always follow the instructions supplied with each piece of equipment and where items of equipment are required to be run-in slowly then you should follow these instructions to the letter.

THE SITE

Too many times houses are completed to a level where the building itself is habitable and unfortunately the site is simply given a quick tidy and the owners move in, but the site remains just that; a building site. The driveway is unfinished, the access

and gateway is unfinished, the landscaping has not been completed and so on. Likely there are a variety of very valid reasons for this to occur, but by far the most common is that the owner has overspent the budget and the only contingency monies are those that were earmarked for landscaping and finishing site works. Do not let this happen to you. Firstly, you should stick to your budget for each aspect of the project and do not be tempted to use monies earmarked for one area to be used for another. If you do fall into this trap, the very last work item is the one to suffer, and that usually means the garden will be finished at some point in the future. Secondly, you should stick to your programme, and make sure that each building element is completed on time, so that the next item can be started on time and so on. Ask yourself the question: 'do I really want my garden to look like a building site for the next few years?' The answer is probably no, so if this is the case,

Finish off hard and soft landscaping while there is still momentum in the project.

you would be better getting the landscaping finished, the garden planted out and any hard surfaces completed while there is still some momentum in the building works.

It is all too easy to move in thinking that come summer again, you will get the garden finished off. The problem is though, that if this is your attitude with external work, it is probably your attitude to other work items internally. In your role as project manager you are the only one who can prevent this from happening to you. Remember: know your budget, then stick to it; know your programme then stick to it. If you move into an unfinished house with an unfinished garden, it will take you four times as long to get the outstanding items finished than if you

had completed the items when they should have been finished. It is always more difficult to go back and try to finish off a job that has been left dormant for a while, than to finish it off at the correct time. Furthermore, it is always more difficult to try to finish off an internal work item when you have moved in and the house is full of furniture, toys and bric-a-brac. Before you even start a job, you have to decant furniture from one room to the next, and so two rooms are now out of commission.

FINANCE AND REGULATION

Financial

In order to obtain the final drawdown on finances,

Resist the temptation to move in until Building Control have issued a completion certificate.

the building must be completed, and to obtain a mortgage there must be some form of completion certificate issued by a source acceptable to the lending institution. Usually, lending organisations require copies of the Building Control Completion Certificate and also a Certificate of Practical Completion signed off by your architect (if they have been retained to inspect the works periodically and certify that they have been carried out generally in accordance with the drawings). Use this final draw-down to pay off all your suppliers and sub-contractors and remember to withhold any agreed retention monies to cover latent defects. Do not be tempted to pay in full any contractor's bill until you are fully satisfied that the work package for which they are responsible has been completely finished. If you have taken out a self-build mortgage, ensure that your mortgage lender is aware of any changes you have made to your house and that they are happy with such changes. It may also be worth shopping around for a better deal on your mortgage, as obtaining a mortgage on a finished house is much easier than on a self-build project. If there are penalties associated with moving your existing mortgage, make sure your new mortgage company will take these on board.

Building Control

Throughout the building process you will have had periodic inspections by the local Building Inspector. Now it is time for your final inspection.

Go through all of the drawings that have been submitted to building control and using these and any other relevant documentation make sure that you have included everything that relates to building control. The local inspector will visit your completed building and make final checks and if everything is in order will issue the completion certificate. This certificate is proof that the local authority considers your house to be generally constructed in accordance with the plans that were submitted to them and stamped approved. If there have been significant deviations from the approved plans, then it is vital that you submit amended plans to building control and have them stamped approved as well. Obviously, building control will only approve plans and construction methods and materials that comply

with the Building Regulations, so ensure that what you have built does indeed comply.

Having built your own house it is not uncommon for owners to do additional building work for which they did not get building control approval. Where this happens, problems often arise when it is time to sell the property because the Building Control Approval does not match what has been built. When this happens you should apply for Building Control Regularisation. The regularisation procedure allows a local authority to consider giving approval to work after it is completed. This power does not replace the enforcement powers already available to the local authority and does not provide a short cut for those who failed to follow the correct procedure. It does mean, however, that if something has been built that does not tie up with the permission granted, then this can and should be put right.

Planning

Having completed your house there should be no reason for you to contact the planning authorities but if for any reason you have deviated slightly from your planning approval, then once again now is the time to get it sorted. Contact the local planner who had responsibility for your original application and explain the situation to them. You probably have a very valid reason for why the house differs slightly from the stamped approved drawings. Have a set of 'as built' drawings prepared and if required, resubmit them to planning. If you are outside the time limit for making minor amendments then you will have to go through the process of submitting a full (retrospective) application again. If the completed project differs only slightly from the approved documents then there should be no problem with obtaining retrospective permission. If, however, you have deviated significantly from the approved drawings, and your house does not comply with the extant policies for that area, then the planning authorities have enforcement powers to demolish, if necessary, offending buildings. It is particularly important to ensure that any conditions that were imposed on the planning permission be carried out to the letter. It is always better to be safe than sorry. If there is something that might be controversial when it comes to selling on your property, then it is better

Ensure the building manual includes instructions for the use of all the built in equipment.

to get it dealt with at this stage than to have potential purchasers put off by minor planning issues that could and should have been sorted on completion.

The Building Manual

The author has worked on a number of commercial projects where at the handover meeting the client has insisted that if the completed building manual is not handed over, then the building itself cannot be handed over. You may be thinking to yourself: 'why do I need a building manual, surely I've designed and built this house and I know every inch of it off by heart?' Chances are though that you do not know everything that needs to be known about all of the systems that you have installed. After a few years you may forget exactly just how everything went together. Furthermore, the manual is probably not so much for you as for others who may be called upon to use or service some of the built-in systems within the house. If they do not have the correct information about the installation, you may be putting their lives at risk. The building manual should contain: drawings, certificates, and operation and maintenance manuals for installed equipment.

The building manual should also contain the energy rating certificate and Code for Sustainable Homes certificate if appropriate.

Drawings

A full set of as-built construction drawings should be placed on file. These are not to be confused with the original and sometimes poorly detailed set of drawings that was produced for building control purposes. While these may be a fairly close approximation of where everything is, they are insufficiently accurate regarding in particular the location of service runs including pipe work, cable runs, access hatchways and others. It is a good idea to undertake a photographic record of everything as you go along. Even if you do not have a drawn record to refer to at least you will have the photographs. Remember to annotate the photographs though, because while you may know what each of the images contain, others no doubt will not have the slightest clue. In a few years time when you want to extend or move an electrical outlet you will find a photographic record invaluable.

Certificates

All certificates issued by your plumber, gas fitter, or electrician should be included with the manual. These should include all commissioning certificates indicating that the installed services are full operational. Include copies of all local authority completion certificates and a copy of the original planning approval. Copies of all operation and maintenance and service manuals should also be included.

MOVING IN

Finally, with all of the above completed, you are ready to move into your new sustainable and energy efficient home and hopefully you can take the time to enjoy the fruits of your hard work. Remember though that your carbon footprint not only depends on how efficient your house is but also on how well you use your new house. Make sure that you know how each of the systems operate and ensure that you use them efficiently.

Time to move in, put your feet up and enjoy the fruits of your labours.

The north elevation with minimum windows.

First floor walls complete.

The building was wind and watertight long before the final cladding was finished.

300mm deep I section engineered roof joists.

wet insulation is then a cold spot inside the wall, which causes further interstitial condensation to occur. Ways to prevent this from happening include very careful sealing of the vapour barrier and locating the vapour barrier in a position where services do not penetrate it. The latter can be achieved by creating a secondary cavity to the inside of the vapour barrier where all of the services will be located. 50mm × 50mm timber battens nailed through the vapour barrier to the inside face of the studs will create such a cavity. Once all of the services have been installed, this cavity can then be filled with insulation to improve the thermal efficiency of the wall.

The Breathing Wall

Another way of overcoming the problem is to place the vapour-resistant sheathing material to the inside face of the studs, and use a material on the outer face that freely allows the passage of any water vapour that finds its way into the insulation. The moisture then dissipates in the outer ventilated cavity. The vapour resistivity of the inner layer should be five times greater then the vapour resistivity of the outer layer. This is called a 'breathing wall' and was chosen for use in this case study.

The breathing wall technology used was a material called 'Fermacel' as the internal wall lining board. The timber frame was made from Masonite 'I' section timber composite members. The outer lining board is a material called 'Bitvent' which is bitumen-impregnated fibreboard. This fibreboard is made from forest thinnings.

The insulation material used is made from recycled newspapers, which is treated with boric salts giving it the required fire resistance and making it vermin proof. The 'Warmcel' insulation is pumped into the cavity between the timber frames after the frame has been erected and the inner and outer skins are in place. Small holes are drilled in the inner (or outer skin) to accommodate the installation, and are then refilled. The principle behind a breathing wall is that it is better to allow the external wall to breathe, by using carefully selected materials, and to allow water vapour to migrate through the wall from the inside to the outside, rather than have a vapour resistant layer on the outside which traps the water vapour within the wall insulation. The Masonite

framing members have a number of advantages over standard solid timber members. There is less material used and they are lighter in weight than solid timber, the cross-sectional area reduces heat loss, and they are much more dimensionally stable than solid members. Unlike standard timber, which has limitations on size, composite timber frame members can be used to create very thick walls, which allow large amounts of insulation to be utilized.

It is the thickness of the insulation which gives rise to the name 'super-insulation'. The Fermacel inner skin is composed of cellulose-reinforced gypsum board. Unlike plasterboard, which has paper skins either side of the gypsum plaster layer, Fermacel has macerated recycled paper throughout the board as reinforcing to the gypsum. The board is almost twice as dense as normal plasterboard and has much greater vapour resistance. This means that water vapour in the house is less able to migrate into the insulation within the wall. However if water vapour does find its way into the insulation, the insulation absorbs the vapour and transmits it to the outer layer of the wall where the Bitvent readily transmits the vapour to outside. An additional layer of building wrap was attached externally to improve air tightness and water resistance until the cladding was installed.

The outside of the house was clad with brickwork on the ground floor to give some robustness and timber cladding was used for the gables, feature panels around windows and a section under the eaves.

If the above wall construction were to be tested against *The Code for Sustainable Homes* it would achieve a rating of five out of a possible six. To achieve code level six using the same materials and wall build-up, the wall thickness would have to increase to 400mm where the additional thickness of insulation improves the thermal performance of the wall.

Floor Construction

Because the house was to be super-insulated it was decided to follow a similar construction method as the walls. Floors were constructed using Masonite joists at 600mm centres, with strips of Bitvent cut to size and resting on the bottom flanges of the Masonite joists utilized to support the floor insula-

Breathable roofing membrane being applied over the sarking boards.

tion. The 300mm depth of the joists required for super-insulation meant that only one supporting wall was required in the centre of the house. Since the house was built on piles and ground beams the requirement for only one supporting wall cut down the cost of under-building significantly. The upper surface of the floor was 22mm water-resistant chipboard throughout.

Upper floors were again constructed using 300mm deep Masonite joists, but this time there was no insulation placed between the joists. The underside of the first floor joists was lined with Fermacel boards to form the ground floor ceiling.

Roof Construction

Once again 300mm deep Masonite joists were used to construct the roof. As the design of the house was a storey and a half, the sloped roof would have to be insulated. This was achieved in the same way as the walls, with the inner skin of Fermacel and the outer skin of Bitvent being installed prior to the cavities between the joists being pumped full of insulation. A Tyvek breathable building membrane was used as the roofing underlay with the roof finish as concrete roof tiles on battens and counter-battens.

This level of insulation in the roof would result in

157

Roof tiles and rooflights fitted.

a *Code for Sustainable Homes* rating of code level three only. To achieve code level six then 450mm joists would have to be used and the cavities between the joists filled with insulation or, alternatively, use a rigid board insulation above and below the 300mm joists. The advantage of the latter method is that all cold bridges would be effectively dealt with.

Minimizing Waste

Note that the overall length of the house has been coordinated to minimize wastage even from the rim joist. The length of the house is the same as the maximum length that can be transported easily on a lorry. This is also the length that the Masonite is supplied in. During the design phase of the project, a cutting schedule was prepared to calculate the number of lengths of Masonite that would be required. Using the short section of the house as a template, one twelve metre length of Masonite was able to be cut to give one wall stud, one floor joist and one first floor wall stud with less than 100mm of wastage from each twelve metre length.

Windows and Doors

Windows were made from treated softwood and obtained from a local joiner. The insulated glazing units comprised two 4mm panes, a 16mm air gap and low-e coating on the inner face of the outer pane. External doors were framed with treated softwood, sheeted with tongue and grooved softwood boards and the resulting cavity between the frames filled with expanded polystyrene insulation to improve the U-value.

U-values and total heat loss

When a house is super insulated, as described above, the heat loss from the building fabric is very low. It is possible to calculate how much heat a house will actually lose by calculating the average heat loss through each of the external building elements of roofs, walls (including an allowance for windows and doors) and the ground floor. The heat loss for each of the building elements is calculated using the U value of the construction build up and is measured in watts per square metre per degree of temperature difference between the inside and the outside (Wm^2degC).

Using a -2°C design temperature externally and 21°C internal temperature, the calculation revealed that the building fabric steady-state heat loss for the whole house would be approximately 2kW only. In theory this meant that a simple two-bar electric fire would only be required to maintain an internal temperature of 21°C when the outside temperature was -2°C providing there were no other sources of heat loss.

Whole House Ventilation

As the building envelope becomes better insulated,

Use of small panes is not as energy efficient as large panes due to the 'edge' effect.

the relative quantity of heat lost though ventilation increases. It is important to note that it not the actual quantity of heat loss that increases since it will stay the same or even decrease, but it is the relative amount that increases. Take for example a standard construction where the ventilation heat loss makes up say 10 per cent of the total heat loss and the building fabric heat loss accounts for say the other 90 per cent. If we were to increase the insulation levels to such an extent that the heat loss through the building fabric became zero, then all other things being equal, the ventilation heat loss now makes up 100 per cent of the heat loss. Thus, as insulation levels increase, ventilation becomes increasingly more important.

Ventilation using Windows

If you are sitting in a house in winter, and trying to maintain a healthy internal temperature of around 21°C, if it is blowing a gale outside and you open a window to let in some fresh air, then you are probably going to feel a draught from the rush of cold air. It is not unusual for people not to open windows in such a situation.

Ventilation using Passive Vents

Another method of ventilating is to use passive vents that are moisture-activated so that they open only when moisture levels inside the house reach a certain level. But once again, it is not uncommon to see houses with their passive vents closed up in winter for the same reason that people do not open windows. If, however, you can control the amount of ventilation and the temperature at which fresh air enters a room then draughts will be a thing of the past.

Whole House Ventilation with Heat Recovery

One way to control the amount of ventilation and the temperature of the ventilation air is to install a whole house ventilation system with heat recovery. The system uses fans to move the ventilation air throughout the house. It works by drawing in fresh air at ambient temperature, passing it through a heat exchanger where it gains heat and delivering the warmed air to the habitable rooms throughout the house. At the same time as fresh air is being delivered to the habitable rooms, another fan is extracting mois-

ture laden stale air from the 'wet' areas in the house such as bathrooms, cloakroom, utility room and kitchen. This already warm but stale air also passes through the heat exchanger (on a different path to the fresh air) on its way to being dumped outside the house, and as it passes through the heat exchanger it transfers heat to the intake fresh air as above. In this way, the majority of heat is recovered and the delivered air, while not quite being at room temperature, nonetheless is tempered to such an extent that it prevents draughts even on the coldest of days.

THE CONSTRUCTION PROCESS

Before Starting on Site

Finance

The bank was informed of operations starting on site and drawdown facilities were put in place.

Neighbours

Neighbours were informed of operations taking place on site. This was done to keep them informed of what and when things would be happening on site. Remember if this is your own house that you are building, then you will have these people as your neighbours for a considerable time.

Site Organization

The site was analysed with regard to: how materials would be delivered; where materials would be stored; where work activities would take place; where scaffolding would be erected – and was laid out accordingly. This is an important aspect of building from both efficiency and also health and safety points of view and should not be left to chance.

Opening Accounts

A number of suppliers, including the local builder's merchants, were approached with regard to opening accounts so that materials could be ordered at trade price. It is important to shop around for materials to get the best price, so having more than one account allows you to compare prices. It also means that if one merchant is in short supply of a particular item, chances are that the other merchant will be able to supply you.

Materials Ordering

A number of materials had to be ordered well in advance of actually commencing operations on site. For example, the Masonite used is manufactured in Sweden, and the Glu-lam ridge beam was manufactured in Norway, and local builder's merchants stocked neither. These were consequently ordered through a stockist in England. It is important to know what materials are going to be used on the project, how much you are going to use (including wastage) and how long the lead times are from placing an order until the materials are delivered to site. Materials that are on the critical path must be delivered on time, otherwise there will be a delay in the overall construction programme. It is better to order a little early and have to store the materials on site than have a delay in delivery. This should be taken into consideration when designing the site layout for operations on site.

Building Control

Building Control were informed that we intended to start on site. They normally require the application number so that they can identify the property. They usually want to inspect the construction at key stages and so were kept informed of progress throughout the building period.

Building Certifier

An architect friend had agreed to inspect and certify the key stages of construction as required by our lending bank. He was informed of the start on site and other key dates to allow him plenty of time to organize site visits.

Insurances

Employer's liability insurance was organized to cover operatives on site should something go wrong

Foundations and sub-structure

Setting-out

Work on site began with clearing scrub from the area where the house was to be located. The setting-out of the house was done by pegging out the outline of the house using the long boundary as the setting-out datum and marking the location of the piles on the ground with lime.

Piling

The piling rig was brought on to the site and the 250mm square reinforced piles were then driven down through the ground fill and into good ground some five metres below the surface where the load bearing capacity of the soil was sufficient to carry the weight of the house.

Ground Beams and Drainage

Next, trenches were excavated in the ground between the piles where the ground beams would be located and a mud mat of 50mm of concrete in the bottom of the trenches provided a working surface on which the block-work permanent shuttering for the ground beams was built. Trenches were excavated for drainage and service routes into the house. The block-work was built to the required depth of the ground beam taking care to ensure that the top of the block-work shuttering was level (so that the top surface of the ground beams would be level). The tops of the concrete piles were broken off using sledgehammers, and the reinforcing cut and bent to help form the pile caps. Reinforcing steel for the ground beams was then prepared and placed in the now shuttered trenches between the piles and tied in place around the pile caps. Drainage pipes and service conduits were put in place where required. Concrete was then poured into the shuttered trenches to the top of the shuttering and vibrated to remove air pockets and ensure that the concrete was properly compacted. The concrete was left for one week to gain some strength before being built on.

Sub-floor Walls

The small sub-floor block-work walls that support the ground floor were then built off the ground beams and once again great care was taken to ensure that the block-work was level. There were a number of sub-floor vents built into these walls to ventilate the void under the floor. Sub-floor ventilation helps to remove ground moisture and any gases that may build up in a confined space.

Sub-floor

50mm of concrete was placed on a polythene damp proof membrane (DPM) on the surface of the

A site on the back doorstep.

that adds thermal mass and will be used to store solar energy. Some steel is used alongside the timber frame to carry heavy loads.

Airtight Construction

One of the key elements of low energy construction is making the building fabric airtight. To achieve this the airtight barrier must be continuous around the whole of the construction and lapped and taped to any components that interrupt the building envelope such as windows and doors. Ensuring the airtight barrier is continuous cannot be left to chance; it must be considered from the beginning of the detailed design stage. The ground floor concrete slab is relatively airtight, however it will shrink through time and gaps will open up. To compensate for this the DPM is carried up the walls and taped to the DPCs,

thus forming an airtight barrier at floor level. The walls are clad externally with a number of layers of Pavatex wood fibreboard with the joints staggered and the external joints sealed with tape.

Because of the built-up nature of the cladding, the wood fibreboards form an effective air barrier. The Pavatex cladding is combined with cellulose insulation between the joists and taped joints on the internal OSB sheathing. In addition, where floors, windows and doors interrupt the airtight barrier, the barrier is lapped and taped to ensure that the barrier is continuous. At ceiling/roof level an Intello breathing membrane is used as the airtight barrier.

Breathable Construction

The overall wall build-up from inside to outside is: gypsum board internal lining; a 50mm cavity filled with hemp fibre insulation; oriented strand board (OSB) sheathing; 'I' section OSB studs with Warmcel cellulose fibre insulation between the studs; Pavatex external cladding and lime render.

The OSB internal sheathing on the inside face of the studs is vapour-resistant and forms the vapour check to the warm side of the insulation. Any moisture that penetrates the OSB layer is transferred through the cellulose insulation and the lime-rendered Pavatex to the outside air. The vapour resistivity of the inner layer is more than five times greater than the vapour resistivity of the outer layer, thus making it a 'breathing wall'.

Floor Construction

The ground floor construction is of solid concrete build-up with insulation above the slab and below the screed. The screed contains heating pipes for underfloor heating. The upper floor is constructed using 300mm deep OSB 'I' section joists, at 400mm centres with the floor deck above glued to the top flange of the joists. The first floor deck will support

Reinforcing mesh in concrete subfloor to prevent cracking (photograph © Mark Forkin, NuTech Renewables Ltd.).

The house nestles into the corner of the tight site to take advantage of evening sun (photograph © Keith Lockhart).

an RTU cement-free screed that once again contains heating pipes for underfloor heating.

Roof Construction

The main roof of the house is a low-slung affair with hipped ends. The roof finish is natural slate with mitred hips on battens on breathable roofing felt on solid timber roof joists. The moisture check/air tightness barrier is fixed to the underside of the joists and gypsum board is the internal finish. Roof insulation is hemp fibre between the roof joists and above the small area of flat ceiling. There is some steelwork supporting the main ridge purlins but the structure is primarily timber. Windows to the first floor are Velux roof-lights and two dormer windows. The windows are timber framed and triple glazed throughout.

The roof over the swimming pool, garage and utility areas is predominantly flat with two large roof-lights. The roof construction build-up is a Trocal roof membrane on a plywood deck on 'I' section OSB joists with flax fibre insulation between joists. The underside has the airtight barrier with gypsum board underneath as the ceiling finish. A sedum green roof finish complements the sustainable credentials of the house.

Minimizing Waste

Every effort has been made to minimize waste

View from the living space out to the courtyard.

including recycling and reusing off-cuts where possible.

Windows and Doors

Windows are proprietary, made from treated softwood from sustainable sources. The insulated glazing units comprise two 4mm outer panes, a 3mm inner pane, and two 12mm air gaps and low-e coatings on the inner face of the outer panes. External doors were framed with treated softwood, sheeted with tongue and grooved softwood boards and the resulting cavity between the frames filled with expanded polystyrene insulation to improve the U-value.

U-values and Total Heat Loss

The U-values achieved in the walls and ceilings/roofs are 0.1 $Wm^2.K$ and 0.1 $Wm^2.K$ respectively.

Whole House Ventilation

Ventilation is achieved using a whole house ventila-

169

The lap pool is an integral component in the thermal hot water storage system.

Ground floor walls constructed using composite timber members (photograph © Keith Lockhart).

Steel framing is used sparingly (photograph © Keith Lockhart).

The walls are clad externally with hemp-lime render on low-density fibreboard (soft board).

Intello breathing membrane over wall heads and under joists.

Hemp-lime render, cellulose insulation between studs and hemp insulation internally.

Cedar cladding on porch and garage walls.

Ground floor ready to receive insulation and underfloor heating in cement-free screed.

First floor joists and flooring will support underfloor heating in cement-free screed.

The sedum roof in full bloom.

tion system with heat recovery to ensure that ventilation heat loss is kept to a minimum.

Water Heating

Water heating is achieved using an 8m² array of evacuated tube solar collectors. The hot water is transferred to a hot water thermal store at first floor level, where it is boosted by a 15kW boiler. The 45m³ lap pool is part of the thermal storage system and stores low grade heat. Underfloor heating at ground and first floor levels is supplied from the thermal store.

Space Heating

Space heating is supplied by underfloor heating pipes buried in the RTU screeds at both ground and first floor levels. The heating is zoned, thermostat and time controlled, and is fed from the thermal store as required.

CASE STUDY 3

Location: Castlebellingham
Designer/Engineer: Mark Forkin
Year Constructed: 2009–2010
Construction Type: Timber frame

Sustainable Technologies Employed:

Passive solar design
Timber frame
Air-tight construction
Whole house ventilation with heat recovery
Evacuated tube solar array
Heat pump

Background

This house is the culmination of many years of research by the owner into passive solar housing in Ireland. Mark is one of the pioneers of passive solar design in Ireland and has built many examples of passive solar houses.

Design Principles behind the Nutech Renewables House

The Nutech Renewables house is based loosely on the principles set out by the Passive House Standard as proposed by the Passivhaus Institut of Germany.

The basic requirements of the 'Passive House' are well established and as follows:

The house should not use more than 15kWh/m² per year of delivered energy for space heating.

After solar gains and incidental gains are taken into consideration, the house should have a specific annual heating load of less than 10 W/m². In respect of air-tightness the air infiltration rate of the house should be less than 0.6 air changes per hour at 50 Pa.

Special attention should be paid to minimize thermal bridging.

Ventilation air should be supplied using a heat recovery ventilation system with an efficiency of more than 75 per cent. The system should be able to supply at least 0.3 air changes per hour of fresh air.

A solar water heating system should be used to supply domestic hot water.

The Nutech Renewables house follows the above principles to a certain degree but it is sufficiently different to be a system in its own right. The concept was devised by Mark and his business partner Bill Quigley.

To start with, the U-values achieved are a little less strict than the German 'Passive House' standard. Mark and Bill maintain that this is because of the law of diminishing returns on increasing insulation levels above what is easily buildable. Put simply, it becomes more and more expensive to achieve less and less in the way of additional gains. To compensate for the lesser performance of the building fabric, the Nutech system uses a larger array of evacuated tube solar collectors to deliver heat into the heat-recovery ventilation system. The advantage of using the slightly more expensive evacuated tube solar collectors over flat plate collectors is that they provide energy even on cloudy days.

The Site

The site is located in the south of Ireland near Castlebellingham. The site is on a slope so some under-building has been used, but the garage to the house is on a split level to reduce the extent of under-build. There are extensive views to the front of the house that have been acknowledged by a large array of glazing in the main living spaces that are orientated towards these views.

Mark's site near Castlebellingham (photograph © Mark Forkin, NuTech Renewables Ltd.).

The House

The house is designed to achieve the same energy rating as the 'Passive House' standard as proposed by the Passivhaus Institut of Germany.

The house is built off traditional strip foundations, with solid floor infill, a solid concrete floor slab and insulation below a traditional sand and cement screed. The screed is designed to act as a thermal store and helps maintain even temperatures all year round.

U-values

The house is based around a traditional timber frame system using 140mm solid timber studs, with 140mm glass fibre insulation between the studs with an additional 50mm of insulation added internally on the warm side of the air barrier. The external wall achieves a U-value of 0.16 W/m^{2}K and the internal insulation is designed to reduce the effect of thermal bridging. Particular attention has been paid to the cold bridging effect of the timber frame, including corner details, and the details around the windows and doors. This is done because the thermal bridging factor of 0.08 W/m^{2}K of standard timber frame construction results in the U-value for all of the elements being increased by this amount. Thus a wall U-value of 0.16 W/m^{2}K becomes 0.24 W/m^{2}K in the overall calculation. Window U-values are 1.2 W/m^{2}K comprising well-designed gas filled double glazing with low-e coatings in hardwood timber frames that are sourced from sustainably managed forests.

Air-tightness

In order to achieve the air-tightness required, as well

177

Foundation walls complete and local stone used as hardcore (photograph © Mark Forkin, NuTech Renewables Ltd.).

as building paper on the outside of the frame, an air barrier is installed on the inside face of the timber panels before they leave the factory.

The air barrier is protected during transport by 50mm × 50mm horizontal battens fixed to the inside of the frames at 600mm centres. The air barrier extends beyond the edges of each wall panel and is either folded back on itself (at the sides of each frame), or wrapped around the wall panel (at the top and bottom of the frame) to provide an overlap when the wall panels are joined together.

There is sufficient overlap at the top and bottom

of the wall panels to allow the air barrier to cross the top of the ground floor frame top wall plate to the outside of the frame where the first floor joists sit, then up the face of the ends of the floor joists or the face of the rim joist to overlap with the bottom of the air barrier of the first floor wall frames. On site the panels are erected in the same way as standard timber frame construction, but care is taken with the air barrier to ensure that it is kept intact and that where two panels meet the barrier is carefully overlapped and the joints sealed with tape. The air barrier is also taped to the window frames.

The solid floor construction is designed to act as a thermal store (photograph © Mark Forkin, NuTech Renewables Ltd.).

Erection of the traditional timber frame wall panels (photograph © Mark Forkin, NuTech Renewables Ltd.).

Factory-installed air barrier at panel ends to ensure continuity at floor and wall junctions (photograph © Mark Forkin, NuTech Renewables Ltd.).

Service Void

The space between the horizontal battens that are fixed to the inside face of the wall panels is used as a service void to run services on site. Where pipe and cable runs are required to run vertically, the air barrier is simply pushed away from the batten, compressing the insulation between the studs a little and allowing the services to pass the batten. In order to maintain the integrity of the air barrier it is important that all of the operatives on site are aware of the importance of not puncturing it. If punctures do occur then these should be taped up

Lapping and taping of the air barrier is crucial to achieving the required airtightness.

Taping of the air barrier to window frames is an integral part of the airtight construction.

using proprietary tape supplied by the air barrier manufacturer for that express purpose. An additional 50mm of fibreglass insulation is then site-applied between the 50mm × 50mm horizontal battens. After this plasterboard is fixed to the inside face of the battens to give the finished wall surface.

Roof Construction

The roof is a traditional timber 'cut' roof (that is, the roof timbers are cut on site) relying on purlins to support the rafters. The roof is made up of a reconstituted imitation slate on battens and counter-battens on a breathable roof underlay, on solid plywood sarking. The whole of the underside of the rafters and sarking is sprayed with a cellulose-based foam insulation (the cellulose is extracted from soya beans. Soya-based foams can have significant shrinkage and because they strongly adhere to the materials to which they are sprayed, they should only be used where the substrate is capable of withstanding the

Additional fibre glass insulation is used internally on the warm side of the air barrier and between rooms for sound proofing.

shrinkage without deforming. Plasterboard has been known to deform under such shrinkage and joints in plasterboard have been known to separate).

The resulting warm roof construction helps maintain air tightness and continuity of insulation around the thermal envelope. One of the problems associated with conventional roof insulation is that roof space vents, when used in conjunction with recessed lighting fixtures and other penetrations through the plasterboard ceiling, create air leakage paths from the warm inside of the house to the cold outside, and vice versa. One further difficulty is that if ductwork

The whole house ventilation system with heat recovery in the cellulose foam insulated roof.

for a heat recovery ventilation system is then placed in the roof space, then the ducts have to be lagged to maintain air temperatures at the correct level. By insulating the underside of the roof sheathing, all of the services in the house including the heat recovery ventilation system are brought inside the thermal envelope, meaning that they are no longer exposed to extreme temperatures.

Overall the level of air infiltration achieves 1.0 ACH at 50 Pa, which is considered by the owner to be a reasonably achievable target that does not have a significant impact on the construction cost.

Ventilation, Space Heating and Domestic Hot Water

A whole house ventilation system with heat recovery is utilized for delivering not only fresh air but also heating. This is achieved by linking a 6m² evacuated tube solar array into the heat recovery ventilation system, so that solar heated air can be circulated to all rooms within the house.

It is worth remembering that evacuated tube solar collectors work even in dull weather. Supplementary heat can be supplied by means of an internal wood pellet boiler or an air-to-water heat pump can also be

The thermal store feeds the underfloor heating system.

Roof lights contribute to high levels of natural daylight.

Flexible flow and return pre-insulated pipes from the solar water heaters at roof level.

integrated into this system. This heat recovery ventilation system is controlled by way of a NuTech intelligent renewable energy system (IRES) controller.

Air Heating

There is also a facility to allow filtered air to re-circulate within the system without passing through the heat exchange, thereby allowing 5 kW to 10 kW of heat to be redistributed. This has the effect of improving the thermal response of the back-up heating system should it be required.

A unique feature of this system is that during periods of higher levels of solar radiation, fresh air is used to ventilate the house (to a higher level than required by the building regulations) using the HRV system. This can be done as it is using the solar array to maintain even internal temperatures with zero energy penalty.

Lighting

Low energy light fittings are used throughout the house and deep plan areas such as halls and staircases are supplied with daylight from rooflights.

Further Information

Health and Safety Executive

http://www.hse.gov.uk/construction/cdm.htm.
The HSE also has a helpline, tel: 0870545500.
Southern Ireland Client Responsibilities publication:
http://www.hsa.ie/eng/Sectors/Construction/

Building Regulations

http://www.buildingcontrol-ni.com/site/default.asp?
secid=home
http://www.sbsa.gov.uk/index.htm
http://www.communities.gov.uk/planningand-
building/buildingregulations/legislation/england-
wales/
http://www.environ.ie/en/

Calculation Tools

The Government's Standard Assessment Procedure
(SAP2005) for individual dwellings under 450 square
metres total floor area.
http://projects.bre.co.uk/sap2005/

The Simplified Building Energy Model (SBEM) for
dwellings with more than 450 square metres total
floor area.
http://www.ncm.bre.co.uk

Register of Approved Certifiers of Construction:

The Scottish Building Standards Agency website:
www.sbsa.gov.uk

Index

A

access   7, 14, 22, 32, 37–41, 44–5, 47, 49, 50,
   55–7, 59, 67–8, 75, 77–8, 94–7, 110, 122,
   136, 143, 148
air barrier   85, 102, 129, 131, 132, 134–35, 156,
   163, 166, 168, 177–8, 180–3
air tightness   85, 94, 101, 129, 132, 156, 163,
   176–7, 181, 183
amenity value   43, 77
archaeologist   22, 39, 50
architect   13, 18–26, 26, 38, 42, 45–7, 49–51, 71,
   75–6, 108–10, 118–9, 133, 146, 150, 161,
   164
autonomous   37, 60–1

B

bank   20, 107, 119, 133, 160, 161
bill of quantities   13, 18, 21, 118–9
boiler   66, 90, 101, 150, 163–4, 176, 184
boundaries   8, 13, 37, 41, 47–8, 50, 56, 120–2,
   165
brief   12–3, 18, 20, 21–2, 25–6, 39, 42, 49–50,
   75–6, 110
budget   12–3, 15, 17–8, 20–2, 25–6, 28, 31,
   37–8, 44, 85, 92, 107–8, 110–2, 117–9, 143,
   145
building control   13–4, 24, 37, 62–3, 85, 95–6,
   98, 99, 101, 103–7, 109–10, 118, 120–1,
   123–5, 131–3, 135–6, 145–6, 148, 152, 161,
   187
building fabric   7, 9, 12, 62–3, 75–8, 80, 86–7,
   94, 100, 103, 116, 124, 150, 153, 159–60,
   163–4, 166, 176
building form   32, 47, 61, 79–80, 94

building manual   28, 143, 147–9
building process   6–8, 14–9, 25, 27, 60–1, 72, 74,
   111, 119–40, 146, 160
building regulations   8, 13, 67, 81, 85, 87,
   95–106, 110, 120, 136–7, 146, 152, 186, 187
building services   20, 24, 37, 61–2, 65, 75, 88–9,
   92–4, 103, 111, 124, 126, 131–2, 134–8,
   142–3, 149, 156, 162, 180, 184

C

carbon footprint   7, 34–5, 70, 149
CDM regulations   18, 28–9, 187
certificates   22–3, 28, 98, 106, 109, 138, 141, 147,
   149
charges   55–6, 112
client 13, 19–20, 22–4, 28–31, 147, 187
climate   6, 8, 39, 40–1, 75, 78, 80, 87
code for sustainable homes   7–8, 12, 61–6, 68,
   148, 156, 158
comfort   6, 25, 78, 164
commissioning   15, 17, 23–4, 28, 99, 103, 121,
   138, 142, 149, 163
completion   11, 15, 17–8, 20, 23–4, 28, 57–8, 72,
   98–9, 105–6, 109–10, 118, 121, 141–9, 165
composting   11, 61, 74, 123
concept statement, 20, 50
conservation   44–6, 48, 61, 95–9
construction   8, 10–20, 22–23, 26–31, 61, 67,
   69–75, 80, 83, 85, 88, 95–6, 99, 103, 106,
   109, 110, 114–5, 119–40, 146, 148, 150, 152,
   156–7, 159–68, 176–179, 182–4, 187
construction process   15, 17, 18, 61, 72, 74, 85,
   109–10, 119–40, 146, 160
contaminated land   22, 30, 39, 41, 111

context 8, 39, 41, 48–50

contours 32, 38, 39, 41

contract 13, 18, 22–4, 30–1, 53–8, 107–119, 132

contractor 134, 18, 21–31, 71, 104, 110–12, 117–21, 125, 132, 136, 146

controls, 61, 93–4, 103–4, 139

coordinate 16, 18, 20, 22, 30, 128, 134–5, 158

covenants 37, 55, 56

cycle 9–10, 60–1, 65, 68, 71, 74, 82–3, 113, 123–4, 140, 156, 164

D

daylighting 8–10, 63, 67, 77–8, 92, 94, 103, 185–6

DER 62–3, 99–100

design consultants 20, 26–7, 31, 38, 43, 45

design costs 108–111, 118

design proposals 20–2, 26, 32, 42, 47, 50, 75, 95, 110

detailed design 13, 18, 22, 47, 49, 109–10, 118–9, 131, 166

DPM 82, 124, 126, 161, 166

drainage 96–7, 111, 116, 121–5, 161

drains 98, 105, 124–5

drawings 13, 18, 20–2, 26–7, 47, 109–10, 117–23, 146–8, 152

dry lining 129, 133–4, 138, 163

drying space 9, 64

E

earth building 69–70,

earth-ship 60–1

earthworks 121, 123

ecological 11, 14–5, 32, 34, 50, 72, 90

ecology 11, 22, 51, 72

electrical 22–4, 28, 87–9, 93–4, 97, 104–6, 116, 121, 134–9, 142, 153, 163

electricity 29, 37, 40, 63–5, 87, 91–2, 111, 136

emissions 7, 9, 15, 62, 64,–6, 75, 81, 99–101, 121

energy efficiency 9, 12, 15, 32, 62–3, 74, 75–103, 164, 176

energy storage 9, 75, 80, 87–91, 94, 101, 176

envelope 9, 61, 63, 73, 75–6, 78, 80–7, 93–4, 100, 103, 115, 117, 130, 141–2, 150, 152, 159, 165–6, 183–4

environmental impact 6, 8, 10–1, 14, 25, 61, 68, 72, 74, 114

estate agents 52–3, 58, 118

excavations 22, 39, 56, 105, 123–4

F

fees 12–3, 18, 23, 108, 110–1, 136

finance 12, 30, 58, 107–21, 145, 150

finishes 121, 126, 138–9, 142

flood 11, 32, 39–41, 48, 66–7, 111

floor 36, 47, 62–3, 68, 70, 72–3, 76, 81–2, 87–8, 99, 101, 105, 122, 124–39, 142, 152, 154, 156–9, 161–8, 171, 174–80, 185, 187

footprint 7, 11, 34–5, 57, 70, 72–73, 113, 123, 149

foundations 32, 56, 72, 105, 110, 121, 123–5, 150, 161, 177

frame 8, 43, 56, 70, 75, 80, 84, 88, 110, 114–5, 120–1, 125, 127–33, 135, 138, 150, 152–3, 156, 158, 162–9, 176–79, 182

G

global warming 7, 9, 62, 66

ground conditions, 22, 32, 38–9, 41, 47, 49–50, 55, 91, 123–4, 131, 150

H

health and safety 13–4, 18 28, 30–1, 58, 95, 98, 111, 120, 122, 124, 160, 187

heat pump 40, 65, 75, 87, 91, 99, 156, 163, 176, 184

heating and ventilation 28, 62–4, 75–6, 80, 87, 89, 91–2, 94, 99, 101, 103, 136, 163–4, 176, 184, 186

history 32, 39

holistic 60–74

home office 9, 65, 67

hot water 65, 75, 87–104, 137, 163–4, 170, 176, 184

I

incidental heat gains 64, 87, 176

initiation 8, 17, 19, 24, 25

insulation 8–9, 63, 66–70, 75, 80–88, 94, 101, 103–5, 114, 125–127, 130–1, 136–7, 150, 152–3, 156–8, 160, 163–9, 173–4, 176–7, 180, 182–3

insurance   22–3, 56, 58, 106, 109, 111, 120–1, 139, 161
integrated   60–1, 89, 91, 186

J
joinery   116, 121, 128, 137, 139, 163–4

L
land value   11, 52–5, 72, 107–8
landscaping   47, 66, 117, 118, 121, 123, 125, 140, 143–5, 164
lifetime   8, 10, 34, 68, 83, 114
lighting 8–9, 63–4, 67, 87, 89, 92–4, 99, 101, 103–4, 136, 139, 183, 186
location   7–8, 13, 20, 25, 33–4, 37–8, 41–2, 47–8, 50, 52, 55–6, 59, 61, 72, 77–8, 122–7, 132, 134–8, 148, 150, 161–2, 164, 176

M
maintenance   98–9, 103, 147
materials   6–7, 9–10, 12–5, 18, 25, 28, 29, 47, 49, 50, 55, 60, 61, 63, 66, 68–9, 71, 74, 78, 81, 83–4, 94, 97–8, 105, 111–25, 129–130, 136–7, 140–1, 146, 156, 160–1, 165, 182
mechanical and electrical engineer   22–4, 88, 104, 137
mortgage   58, 107–9, 146

O
occupation   24, 28, 68, 105, 118, 164
openings   80, 83–5, 103, 128–9
orientation   32, 38, 61, 77–8, 94, 103
outline design   12, 21–2
ownership   8, 39, 47, 55

P
party wall   37, 56, 59
passive solar design   12, 60, 75, 77, 78, 80, 85–7, 90, 93, 103, 150, 160, 164, 176–7
planner   13, 22, 26, 32, 38–9, 42, 43, 45, 48–9, 52, 146
planning   12–3, 17, 20, 21–2, 245, 27, 29–30, 37–59, 80, 96, 107, 109, 120–2, 146–152, 164, 187
plant hire   27–8, 117–8
plaster   70, 105, 110, 112–3, 116, 128, 134, 136–40, 153, 156, 182, 183

policy   41, 43–4, 46, 48–51, 164
pollution   9, 11, 15, 60, 62, 65–6, 72, 74, 82
prefabrication   131
pressure testing   99, 103, 125
programme   12–3, 15, 17, 20, 23, 25–6, 28, 30–1, 109, 112, 117–21, 140, 143, 145, 161
project management   15, 17–31, 71, 108

Q
quantity surveyor   18, 21–4, 110, 118

R
renewable energy   9, 12, 32, 40–1, 44, 49, 62, 75–6, 83, 87, 90–2, 115, 176, 177, 186
reserved matters   47
responsible sourcing   10, 68–9
roads consultant   22, 110
roof   9–11, 50, 60, 62–3, 65–8, 70–3, 76, 81, 83, 98, 101, 105, 114, 124–7, 131–3, 136, 141, 146, 153, 155–9, 161–3, 165–9, 175, 182–6
R-value   81

S
SAP   98–100, 104, 187
security   10, 28, 72, 108, 139
setting-out   122–3, 127
setting-up   121
shelter   32, 40, 75, 78, 94, 110
site analysis   12, 32–3, 37, 41–2, 49–50, 77, 109–10
site costs   108, 110–2
solar access   32, 38, 40, 41, 75, 77–8, 94
solar energy   12, 32, 401, 60, 65, 75, 77, 80, 85, 87, 89–94, 99, 103, 164, 166, 176, 186
solar radiation,   77, 94, 186
solar water heater   65, 87, 90, 91, 186
solicitor   20, 55–9, 118
sound   9, 41, 57, 67, 97, 183
space heating   62–4, 76, 80, 87, 89–91, 94, 100, 103, 136, 176, 184
stove   90
straw bale   70
structural engineer   18, 22–3, 26
sub-contractors   13, 18, 22–4, 28, 110–2, 117–118, 121
surface water run–off   11, 15, 66

sustainability   6–8, 12, 32–4, 37, 41, 60–2, 68, 81, 90, 98, 114, 130

T
tender   13, 18, 22, 27, 31, 58, 107–19
timber   26, 32, 50, 69, 70–1, 75, 80, 83, 88, 98, 110, 113–5, 120–40, 150, 152–3, 156, 162–6, 168, 171, 177, 178, 179, 182
title   20, 47, 556, 58–9, 87, 106
topography   8, 32, 38, 41, 48, 50
tree preservations orders   57

U
user guide   10, 15, 71, 101
utilities   26, 32, 37, 41, 61, 123
U-value   63, 81, 99–101, 104, 158–9, 169, 176–7

V
valuer   20, 52
VAT   15, 108, 112, 117–8,

ventilation   15, 28, 61–4, 75–8, 80, 85–7, 89, 91, 94, 96–7, 99, 101, 103, 125, 128, 132, 134, 136, 150, 159–64, 169, 176, 184, 186

W
walls   37, 50, 56, 59, 61, 63, 67–72, 76, 78, 80, 84, 88, 101, 105, 124–38, 152, 154, 156–7, 159, 161–3, 166, 169, 171–3, 178
waste   7, 11, 14–5, 60–1, 66, 72–4, 80, 122, 140, 158, 168
water   9, 11, 15, 28, 37, 39–40, 47, 50, 60–7, 72–8, 81, 83, 85, 87–92, 94, 97, 99, 101, 104, 109–11, 116, 124–8, 130, 132–8, 150, 153, 155–7, 163, 164, 170, 176, 184, 186
welfare facilities   29, 30, 122
wellbeing   9, 15, 67
working drawings   13, 22, 27, 118–21

Z
zero carbon   7, 9, 63, 65, 82, 99–100

Related titles from Crowood

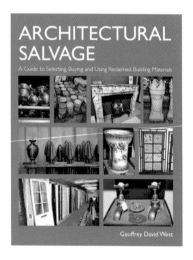

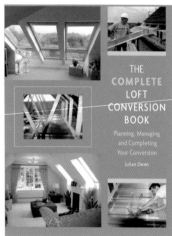

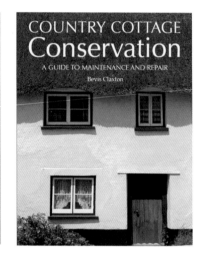

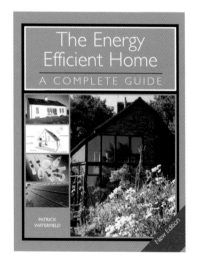

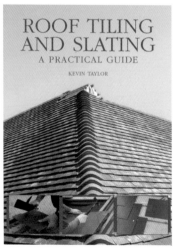

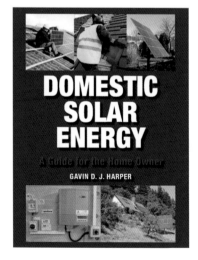